Quantum Origins

Keys for Ancient Cosmology

Michael Garber

MICHAEL GARBER

Printed in the United States of America
First Printing 2021
First Edition 2021

Second Edition

ISBNs:
Softcover 978-1-959561-05-7
eBook 978-1-959561-06-4

10 9 8 7 6 5 4 3 2 1

THE
ILLUMINATION
CODEX

Table of Contents

ACKNOWLEDGMENTS

I bow in humble recognition of the One Light of Consciousness, the Source of my being and the source of all knowledge and wisdom. I give gratitude to the Supreme for dreaming me into existence and allowing me to have the conscious experience of life and the crafting of this codex.

I bow in love and gratitude to my dear beloved partner Ron Amit, a true gift of the Divine, for all the many ways he supports me in my life. I am blessed beyond measure to have such a brilliant master of love, compassion, and divine service to walk this earthly life with. Thank you for all that you do, seen and unseen, to amplify joy and higher consciousness for me and all beings in the Cosmos. I love you across all space, time, and dimensions.

I send gratitude to my friends and clients who have brought forth the lost stories of Creation through their Illuminated Quantum Healing hypnosis sessions. Thank you for being the powerful Light beacons that you are!

I send deep gratitude to my many modern scribes who assisted me in the transcription work. Thank you for helping me capture these incredible client stories so that the world can remember our cosmic divine heritage.

Bless all the beings, seen and unseen, who have helped me craft this material so that you, the reader, can be nourished on your path of Ascension. May you, the reader, be blessed infinitely and discover the highest truth of your being. May ascended consciousness, liberation, and divine unification be yours in this very life!

DEDICATION AND INVOCATION

This book is dedicated to the infinite expressions of our Oneself, for the celebration of our many incarnations, past, present, and future, and the lessons we have learned throughout eternity. May these words and the energy they carry be a potent force for awakening for all seekers of Unconditional Love and divine Truth. May this transmission support the reactivation and restoration of humanity's divine blueprint upon planet Earth and accelerate the realization of our eternal unity and oneness with all of Creation.

Let us join in prayer, honoring and sending gratitude to the Supreme Intelligent Source of Creation, the omniscient, omnipotent, omnipresent, transcendental Divine Source that is our True Nature.

Let us honor and send gratitude to the higher Light realms and the beings of Light who guide and protect Creation's evolution. Let us honor and send gratitude to our star lineages and those who support us from beyond the Earth. Let us receive your love and blessings now as we remember our cosmic ancestry and our role in the higher evolutionary plan for Creation.

Let us honor and send gratitude to our Earth Mother and her many dimensions and manifestations of Life including the animal, plant, bacterial, fungal, protozoan, mineral, crystalline, and elemental beings who contribute to her dynamic, regenerative biomes. These writings are offered as salve and balm to heal and bless our beloved Gaia, our Earth Mother and Divine Sister. May her waters be pure, her soil rich, her air clean, and may all beings, seen and unseen, within her living biofield know lasting peace forever and ever.

Let us honor and send gratitude to the wisdom and guidance from the seven directions of East, South, West, North, Above, Below, and Within. Let us call back our soul fragments scattered through time and space so that we may anchor ourselves HERE and NOW in this eternal moment of infinite potential to witness the unfolding manifestation of the Divine Plan.

Let us honor and send gratitude to the elements of Earth, Air, Fire, Water, and Ether that create the foundation of our evolutionary experience in form. May the Light of Consciousness awaken swiftly in each of us as we remember our True Nature beyond names and forms.

Let us honor and send gratitude to our ancestors and the many souls who have shared their light upon the Earth. Let us send special thanks to those who dedicated their lives to passing on the Mysteries and sacred knowledge of the Divine so that we may NOW stand at this Grand Turning of the Ages, with the support of all who have come and all who are destined to live upon this great Earth.

I call forth the full remembering of our divinity and the weaving of a new story of harmony and peace for all of Life upon the Earth. May we shed our stories of limitation and suffering and step forward into a new era as People of Light, cosmic co-citizens, and ambassadors for the Living Light of Creation.

Hallelujah! Jai! Aho! Blessed Be! Amen! And so, it is! Om!

GUIDANCE FOR READING THIS BOOK

The Illumination Codex is a multidimensional library for the path of Ascension. It is holographic by nature as each chapter contains a multitude of keycodes to activate ancient cellular memory and trigger multidimensional awareness and higher consciousness integration. As you read the material, your Inner Being will offer flashes of insight and higher perception into your awareness to assist you in healing, spiritual activation, and cosmic remembrance. I recommend using a highlighter, journaling your process, and using other resources to research and enhance your understanding of the topics presented in this book.

A major influence for this material comes from my work as a past-life regression hypnotherapist using the methods we have codified into a technique called Illuminated Quantum Healing (IQH). While in a deep hypnotic trance, my clients experience other lifetimes and other planetary civilizations and communicate with advanced intelligent species from beyond the Earth and Earth plane. The information contained in this book is a summary of my understanding of all that I have learned through my clients as they journeyed to the ancient past, probable timelines of the future, and higher planes of Light. There are many transcriptions of IQH sessions included in the book for you to have your own unique interpretation and multidimensional experience with the material.

This book contains a diverse collection of spiritual information from a variety of wisdom traditions that I have studied in my life. These writings are my own interpretations and understandings of these different concepts that have helped me in my awakening journey and do not necessarily speak for the lineages themselves. This presentation of information is meant as a collection of keys to unlock the wisdom that is already encoded within you. None of it is meant to become dogmatic as consciousness revelation and ascendency will open us continuously to higher and higher truths and understanding.

I confess that I share this transmission as a fellow traveler on the path of awakening. I have my own limitations, my own egoic nature, and my own struggles. I am capable of error and ignorance just as any other person. This presentation of information is what I have found along my path which has triggered awakening and helped me on my path back home to my Self. My prayer is that this book will become deeply meaningful for you and be a guiding light back to your own liberated being.

While reading this material, you may come across something in the text that triggers something within you that is uncomfortable. Maybe it is words that I use, perspectives that I share, or something else that may bring up resistance, judgment, anger, guilt, and so on. This is a wonderful opportunity to investigate the origin of the reactive mental and emotional patterns that create such experiences. The origin may come from earlier stages of your life or previous lifetimes. Use this as an opportunity to reconcile those parts of your consciousness through spiritual inquiry and self-study so that you may realize deeper states of wholeness and clarity.

This text is intended to activate 'gnosis,' a direct experience and knowledge of the divine presence within and around you. I do not recommend blind faith in any concept or religious doctrine. The information in this book is not meant to be treated as religious dogma that cannot be questioned or developed further. It is meant to be utilized to unlock the truth that lives within your very being. I am not writing this intending to change people's beliefs or convert anyone. I am simply relaying the summary of my life's research on the quest for spiritual truth. If something from the material does not resonate as truth in your heart, release it and move on to the next part of the transmission. Use the philosophy and information in this text to stimulate your expansion and the embodiment of YOUR deepest truth and to strengthen your relationship and innate connection with the Divine.

Another thing to mention is capitalization. You will notice that there are words that are not normally capitalized in other books and sacred texts that are capitalized in this text. My intention behind this was to add spiritual dimensionality to words that describe qualities or names of the Divine.

Typically, when I speak of light in this book, I am speaking about higher-dimensional, intelligently-encoded subtle energy and not conventional light from a light bulb. When I speak about "energy," I am speaking about subtle energy which exists beyond the visible light spectrum for most people. Many are becoming sensitive to subtle energy (i.e., multisensory, intuitive, psychic) and are developing the ability to sense and perceive this energy through extrasensory perception. All of humanity is evolving towards being able to perceive and interact with subtle energy and higher cosmic intelligence and consciousness.

The use of the term consciousness fluctuates throughout the book and can mean different things. When I speak of pure Consciousness I am speaking about your True Self as Source Consciousness, the Absolute, the Eternal Witness of all Creation, pure Awareness and Existence itself. Other times I will speak of consciousness as in variations of the mind such as unity consciousness or separation consciousness. All forms of consciousness, all experiences of the mind, borrow existence from the One Light of Consciousness and you are that!

I tried my best to organize this text in a way that can be read from front to back like any regular book, but it can also be read any way you feel intuitively called to read it. Part of the reason for the size of this codex is because it is difficult to explain one part without understanding many other components. In my effort to answer all potential and probable questions about ascension, I wrote everything I could on this multifaceted, multidimensional topic.

As you make your journey through this material, there are three stages to help integrate the information and use it to fuel your awakening to your True Nature:

Stage One: Listening (*Sravana*) As you read or listen to the material in this book, allow it to penetrate deeply and work with your inner philosophical understanding. Listen deeply to your Inner Being for there will be flashes of insight and knowing that emerge within your inner consciousness space.

Stage Two: Reflection (*Manana*) Try your best to understand the information contained in this book through self-inquiry and inner philosophical pondering. I am not asking for you to blindly believe any of this transmission. Think of this information as an active hypothesis. You do not have to believe it, but you can reflect over the information and see how it applies to your life.

Stage Three: Integration/Meditation (*Nididhyasana*) As you take in the words in stage one and convert the words to knowledge and understanding in stage two, you move into conviction and integration of knowledge in stage three as you crystallize and embody the Self-knowledge of "I am Pure Consciousness." As you go about your daily life, use the knowledge you have gained to interrupt habit and conditioned thought and re-direct your mind toward the Light of Consciousness that you are.

Gateways of Entry

Besides reading front-to-back or intuitively hopping around, I have created six gateways for you to enter the presentation of the material. I have created one large book that has all of the Illumination Codex material and separated the material into separately published volumes to make the information more digestible. The Gateways are as follows:

GATEWAY ONE: ASCENSION INITIATION: KEYS FOR HIGHER EVOLUTION gives an overall understanding of Ascension, reincarnation, universal law, and a theoretical and philosophical framework concerning Cosmic Evolution. This is an excellent place to start if you are open and eager to learn about these subjects and awakening, you may want to start in Gateway Three.

GATEWAY TWO: AKASHIC DATABASE contains a wide variety of Illuminated Quantum Healing session transcriptions describing key figures and events in the history of Creation, galactic history, ancient planetary history, and probable future timelines of New Earth from clients in hypnotic visionary states. This is a suitable place to enter the material if you already have a general understanding of multidimensionality, galactic civilizations, and the process of personal and planetary ascension. This gateway is conveniently separated into QUANTUM ORIGINS, COSMIC CHRIST TRANSMISSIONS, and NEW EARTH TRANSMISSIONS. If you find yourself resistant to those ideas and are new to these subjects. I recommend developing a meditation practice parallel to reading this material as the transcripts are deeply activating on multiple levels.

GATEWAY THREE: PATH OF AWAKENING: KEYS FOR TRANSFIGURATION is an in-depth collection of spiritual and philosophical wisdom to support personal, relational, and planetary healing. If you are in the beginning stages of awakening or moving through a deep healing process, you may wish to start here so you can develop your consciousness and prepare your mind and body for higher level initiation into the Mysteries.

GATEWAY FOUR: CHAKRA YOGA DISCOURSE transmits deeper

insight into the themes and physio-psycho-spiritual domains of the vortices of life force and perception called the *chakras*. Each section transmits valuable information to understand the common distortions in these processing centers and how to activate and reconcile each center.

GATEWAY FIVE: LAYING HANDS: REIKI & BEYOND is a full manual for learning the art of the laying of hands for healing. The manual clearly describes all the stages, steps, and practices to perform powerfully transformative hands-on-healing sessions for yourself, others, and even in groups. This manual would be acceptable for any Level 1 and Level 2 Reiki course.

GATEWAY SIX: ASCENSION LEXICON is a glossary of commonly used words to describe the process of awakening and ascension. These definitions act as keycode activators to unlock deeper meaning and inner wisdom. Many words used in spiritual/ascension circles are convoluted and sometimes lose their impact because they are misused or misunderstood. I may use words in a way you are not familiar with, or I may use words differently than you. I tried my best to make a glossary with foundational vocabulary to assist with understanding the material. You may wish to read the ASCENSION LEXICON before journeying through the main text of the book.

Bless you on your personal path through this material. May the light in your heart guide you with ease and grace on your journey of initiation with *The Illumination Codex*.

ABOUT THE AUTHOR
Awakening to the Quantum Reality

In the Summer of 2016, I was given a book that forever changed my life's direction called *The Three Waves of Volunteers and the New Earth* by Dolores Cannon. This book was a huge catalyst in my spiritual awakening. Reading the text stirred something deep within me and resonated profoundly with my heart's truth. The book's pages sent waves of energy down my spine as I began to awaken to a higher consciousness reality and remember my purpose for being born upon the Earth at this time.

Dolores Cannon was a world-renowned hypnotherapist specializing in past-life regression. To understand the power of regressive hypnosis, we also need to understand the workings of the mind. The mind can be separated into three categories: the conscious mind, the subconscious mind, and the superconscious mind.

The conscious mind is the ego/personality part of the mind. This active part of the mind uses limited information from the environment and past experiences to make decisions and take care of the body.

The subconscious mind is the recording device of our mind. It records incredible amounts of information at every moment. We easily pull data from the subconscious when we think about something from our past as we access memory.

Deeper in the subconscious, sometimes called the unconscious mind, we have unconscious memories and information, including societal conditioning, painful traumas from this life that are too painful to remember, and memories from other lifetimes. Even though this information is not in the conscious mind, it silently influences our day-to-day experience as reactive emotional momentum, called *samskaras* in Sanskrit, from past events which overlay and filter our experience of the present moment. These subconscious patterns are like applications running in the background of smartphones that quietly drain the processing speed and battery, silently influencing processor speed and functionality.

The superconscious mind is a higher mind capacity that gives us access to intuitive information, extrasensory perception, non-local consciousness, creative genius, universal connection, and access to divine consciousness. This part of the mind is mostly undiscovered and underdeveloped in most of humanity.

Dolores created a unique method of hypnosis, Quantum Healing Hypnosis Technique (QHHT), that opened a doorway to the client's subconscious mind to explore other lifetimes and realms in Creation. When I use the word "quantum," I am speaking to the fabric of Consciousness, the multidimensional unified field of Creation. When clients are in these hypnotic states, they tap into the part of their consciousness that is nonlocal and connected to All That Is. This includes access to other lifetimes, other realities and dimensions, and other intelligent consciousness forms (i.e., higher-dimensional light beings, telepathic extraterrestrials, etc.). Through this experience, clients came to understand another perspective and origin of self-sabotaging and limiting beliefs that were playing out in this life and the core mental/emotional patterns that create illness and disease.

During her sessions, Dolores started to contact a part of her clients' consciousness that seemed to have endless knowledge and wisdom. She called this aspect of her clients the Subconscious or the SC. Others have called this the Higher Self, the oversoul, superconsciousness, or the cosmic consciousness. I prefer the term Higher Self and superconscious mind and go into great detail of how to activate and evolve superconsciousness throughout this text. While the information was limitless, the SC/Higher Self would only answer questions in a way that was appropriate for the client's learning path and honored their free will. When working with the SC, both Dolores and the client described powerful healing energy in their bodies and the treatment room. Clients often reported instantaneous healing as they were transformed from the inside out during the session. While this may seem too good to be true, there are countless documented and measurable occurrences where clients received lasting miraculous healing through these types of sessions.

When she would work with the Higher Self, this higher consciousness identity and supportive Light team would speak through the client as a collective consciousness as if the client were speaking in third-person perspective about themselves. "We are always guiding her. We wish she would follow her intuition more." and "We are beginning to use white light to heal this now." are common examples of how "They" (i.e., SC/Higher Self) express themselves and heal the client during the session.

The healing work is always done with unconditional love and honors the free will and sovereignty of the client. If instantaneous healing was not "appropriate" for the client's growth and spiritual maturation, "They" would suggest what steps the client should take to heal themself. Slowly, over many years, Dolores's work expanded as "They" introduced more components to the healing process so that she could evolve her work and teach it to others.

The Three Waves of Volunteers and the New Earth was one of nineteen books written by Dolores Cannon before her transition out of physical life. Each book contains transcriptions of client sessions describing detailed events from other lives while using her Quantum Healing Hypnosis Technique (QHHT).

Awakening to the Starseed Volunteer Mission

After several years of working with clients worldwide, Dolores noticed a pattern of clients describing a massive galactic and higher dimensional mission to raise the vibration of the planet and shift it into a new reality called the New Earth. The book describes how countless numbers of advanced spiritual beings from distant star systems, and even other universes, volunteered to incarnate on the Earth with a mission to raise consciousness on the planet and assist with this grand transition.

The New Earth is a higher frequency Earth reality that exists in a higher dimension than we are in now. Clients describe a large-scale plan initiated by Source Intelligence (God) to reset life on planet Earth back to the original template of a harmonic environment thriving within diversity. Parallel to this, Dolores's work described a shift in human consciousness from a duality-based mindset to a heart-centered, multidimensional consciousness and a less physical body of light.

The First Wave Volunteers were born beginning around 1945 through the 1970s. They were like a stealthy reconnaissance mission. First on the scene. First to patrol and feel out the collective consciousness vibrations. First to introduce the higher consciousness perspectives to the masses. Many had a difficult and lonely time since there were not many other humans in higher, love-based spiritual consciousness on the planet at the time.

The Second Wave Volunteers were born around the late 1970s through

1990s and are channels for higher spiritual energy and divine wisdom. These souls came in with a higher level of intuitive gifts and are often extremely sensitive to energy. Many are hands-on healers, musicians, vocalists, yoga teachers, and so on. They are space-holders who transmit a new frequency out to the field of Earth, bridging the old ways with the new ways and consciousness of New Earth.

The Third Wave Volunteers, the younger generations, are builders and innovative geniuses in science, spirituality, technology, and so on. They are divinely inspired visionaries that will build the New Earth. They are radical lovers and shine bright with crystalline eyes and have achieved high consciousness levels in other lifetimes. Some of these souls have never had a physical incarnation or have come straight from Source as new souls with pure Light and no karma.

I have been told all the children born at this time are part of this Grand Mission. They are pure souls, evolutionary masters, here to build the New Earth. More is written about the Starseed Mission and phenomena later in this book.

As I was reading Dolores's book, I felt I was reading my own story. I felt the truth in her words. Suddenly so many things made sense about my life. I finally had answers to why I felt so different from others in my community and family. I understood why I felt other people's emotions and could tell what people were thinking. It all started to click together. I was so excited to share the book with Ron, my husband and co-founder of New Earth Ascending, who also deeply resonated with the material.

At the same time, we were beginning to work with an Australian musical group as dancers for their "Return of the Bird Tribes" tour for their album by the same name. Something about the term "bird tribes" caught my attention, and I started to research it. I found the book by the same name, written by Ken Carey, in 1988 that describes a prophecy of high spiritual beings returning to the Earth at a time of spiritual renewal.

Many cultures describe times when culture-bringing beings would come from the heavens or from across the waters to bring technology and information to humanity throughout history. Thoth went to the Egyptians, White Buffalo Calf Woman went to the Native Americans, Quetzalcoatl went to the Aztecs, the Seven Sisters of the Pleiades went to the Aboriginal people of Australia, beings from the Sirius A and B binary star system went to the Dogon people of Mali; and many other stories exist in many other cultures. Carey's book described when these beings would come again during a time of spiritual awakening on the planet.

I was receiving information from multiple directions and was going through a massive realignment with my soul's purpose as I became aware of this greater story and mission. Ron and I went to an arts festival in the desert of Nevada called Burning Man. While we were there, a couple excitedly recognized us as "twin flames" and asked us which star system we had come from. "We are from Sirius. Where are you from? Orion? The Pleiades? Sirius?" she asked. The concept of "starseeds" and "twin flames" was new to me, and I did not know what to say. I saw a special sparkle in the couple's eyes and felt that I should do some research to understand more about it.

After some research and some magical synchronicities, Ron convinced me that we should do the QHHT training and certification process. I was super resistant to learning it because of deep religious programming and egoic structures that made me doubtful of the truthfulness of the work. I was familiar with reincarnation but did not necessarily believe in it. Eventually, I gave in to Ron's suggestion and took the QHHT course.

Evolving Beyond QHHT

In the early stages of practicing QHHT, Ron and I were guided to start doing the sessions online to share the technique's power with as many people as we could. This method was not permitted by the organization because Dolores did not believe it to be safe and her organization does not permit it still. Dolores was an elder and this type of technology was new to her, whereas the younger generations are much more comfortable interfacing with video conferencing.

We have been told by the Higher Consciousness that there is nothing to fear, and NOW is the time to spread these healing methods across the world in whatever way is possible. To honor our lineage and teacher, we stopped using the name QHHT and started experimenting with different names as our way of practicing quantum healing evolved beyond our initial training.

Online sessions are just as powerful as in-person sessions and are often more comfortable and affordable for the client. It is completely safe to facilitate sessions remotely, and we have had countless powerful sessions that have been facilitated in this way. Dolores's organization does not allow adaptation of the QHHT technique. Its practitioners need to perform the method exactly how Dolores taught and not add any modifications or outside techniques. While it is important to protect the work's integrity, this rigidity does not permit the work to expand to its full potential. We are in a time of expansion and evolution, and we must always be open to the transformation and progression of all methods we currently use or risk leaving them in the past as everything on the Earth is evolving.

Another topic that caused us to evolve beyond our initial training of QHHT was the organization's strict denial of negative spiritual attachment and what felt like shaming those who believed in this common experience. Ron and I and other quantum healing practitioners discovered that certain psychological, emotional, and physical imbalances were being created by pervasive energies that did not belong to the client's energy field that had somehow become attached to the client. This includes spirit attachments, curses from past lives, and implants from nefarious beings to name a few. QHHT did not provide us with appropriate training to work with these serious complications. If it were found out that a practitioner had adopted these practices and still operated under the name of QHHT, practitioners could be removed from the QHHT directory.

Many practitioners have reported spontaneous visitation from Dolores through clients under hypnosis where she has encouraged practitioners to follow their intuitive guidance and continue to develop the work through experimentation just as she did when she developed QHHT.

We were inspired greatly by other quantum healing practitioners' extraction methods and crafted our own approaches to clearing pervasive energies and spirit attachments. The reality of negative thought-forms, negative extraterrestrial implants, and entity attachment is too big to ignore, considering so many cases are emerging, not to forget the thousands of years of wisdom and extraction practices passed down by Indigenous peoples and various wisdom traditions.

We never assume that someone has an entity just because they suffer, and we do not bring it up in our intake interview. Once the client is deep in a hypnotic trance, we ask the Higher Self if there are entities or attached energies. If the answer is yes, then we ask questions to understand how this occurred and if the client has anything to learn to release negative attachment. From there, the Higher Self can immediately extract the energy and take it back into the Light for healing. It is all extremely safe, insightful, and benefits all who are involved. We have found that, often, the revelation of spirit attachment or implants will not occur unless the practitioner asks and gives permission for a scan specifically for attached energies. Ron and I believe this is because of the honoring of the free will of the entities involved in the experience of attachment.

In my opinion, to continue to deny such experiences is a disservice to the clients who come to us seeking answers and healing. All practices and traditions can become dogmatic if we do not allow the evolution of thought to take us into new frontiers of consciousness. These are evolutionary practices, and we need to be constantly open to shifting our paradigm so that we can offer the best guidance and support with the changing of times.

Once we started offering quantum healing sessions online, clients started coming to Ron and me from all over the world. Not only were the sessions powerfully healing and transformative for the clients, but we were also going through a rapid transformation as we learned about ancient stories and galactic events from the perspective of souls embodied at those times. While Dolores taught that many people had "potato-picking lives," simple lives with simple themes, it seemed that almost every session of mine had to do with the New Earth Mission, powerful events from the ancient past, and future timelines of Earth.

I soon realized that I was getting a theme and timeline in my sessions. The timeline given to me via my clients describes how Creation came into being, ancient galactic history, the seeding of life on Earth, the rise and fall of ancient civilizations, the true teachings of Jesus through the eyes of people that were closest to him, information about the transformation of the human body to a less dense body of Light, and the evolution of the Earth into the higher frequency reality of New Earth. In less than a year, I went from a reincarnation skeptic to believing that anything is possible, and that the multiverse is more incredible than we can even imagine!

Illuminated Quantum Healing

After years of practicing and evolving how we do this work, Ron and I have created our own quantum healing method that incorporates all that we have learned on our path. This includes facilitating sessions online to reach as many people as possible to assist in this Great Awakening.

Our training method acknowledges spirit attachment and teaches our facilitators how to perform negative spirit releasement. We teach yogic psychology, holistic wellness concepts, and energy healing methods to ensure the practitioner has a thorough understanding of human consciousness and how to lead the client through the ascension process using multiple IQH sessions and mentorship programs. We call our method Illuminated Quantum Healing. IQH can be learned in live classes or through our online course offered on our social network Source⊙Energy.

Illuminated Quantum Healing (IQH) is a personal transformation method for multidimensional holistic healing and consciousness development. IQH incorporates energy healing, meditative practices, yogic philosophy, and hypnosis skills to reconcile limiting subconscious patterning and integrate instantaneous multidimensional healing and wisdom from one's Higher Self.

I am deeply honored to be a part of this work. I am so blessed to have an opportunity to work with such incredible people and energies. Each session that I facilitate nourishes me to the core, and I have the sublime opportunity to observe miraculous instantaneous healing and transformation in my clients. After witnessing the infinite potential of quantum healing hypnosis, I firmly believe that we can ascend beyond all states of illness and disease and that we have infinite support to move beyond the shadows of our past and become a new People of Light.

Getting to the New Earth involves a process of spiritual growth and purification. To transition with the Earth, it is required that we raise our vibration to match the accelerating frequency of the Earth as it changes. Mostly, this is about releasing fear and negative karma. I have written this book as a tool to use for your spiritual awakening and transformation that many are calling Ascension. This is my gift to humanity to help make the process easier and explain different components to cultivate a deeper understanding of this Grand Shift to New Earth and our newly evolving Lightbody.

Spiritual awakening and ascension are available for ALL people no matter what they have done in their past, current economic status, gender expression, sexuality, religion, etc. There are as many paths to the New Earth as there are humans on the planet. No one religion holds the keys or the way to heaven. The power is within YOU!

To support the global ascension process, we have created New Earth Ascending. New Earth Ascending is a non-profit, faith-based organization focused on global ascension and establishing heart-centered, sustainable communities and educational centers around the world.

Alongside Illuminated Quantum Healing (IQH), Ron and I have created other pathways of support for the global ascension process:

1. Embodied Light Reiki Training and Certification

2. New Earth Ascending has three levels of Reiki certification to train people how to channel divine light for healing. These trainings honor the lineage and teachings of the Usui System of Natural Healing while also infusing evolutionary concepts and practices that go beyond standard Reiki training.

3. Online courses for awakening and ascension are available on our private social network Source⊙Energy. The courses include philosophical exploration on several models of spiritual growth and alchemical practices to support your healing, awakening, and ascension. These courses include meditations, holistic wellness education, breathwork, lightbody activation and more. These courses lay foundational understanding for beginners and move through a progression of intermediate and advanced practices and knowledge.

4. TransformOtion was created to support the embodiment of one's Higher Self using dance, somatic movement, yogic practices, meditation, imagination, and energy healing. This fusion of practices helps to purify and repair the physical, etheric, and mental bodies so that one can move beyond perceived limitations into boundless rhythm and flow. Through this interweaving of multiple disciplinary paths, we integrate physicality with transcendental ecstatic play while cultivating a deep connection with and trust in the body's wisdom.

These ideas and concepts can be used for personal embodiment and activation or infused into performance art to create powerful alchemical experiences for the performer and the audience. This fusion of high art and spiritual transformation creates a multidimensional experience for all who are within the field of performance energies.

5. Source⊙Energy is a social network exclusively for those on the path of ascension to connect and share inspiration as we manifest and build a New Earth. We invite all souls who feel aligned with New Earth to join this network and add your unique energy and love to this community. Source⊙Energy serves as a pathway of social interaction and is the home of our online courses and training.

6. Children are our future. Youth inspiration and enrichment programming is in development to assist the spiritual activation and consciousness mastery of the youth. NEA is dedicated to creating harmonic environments and rich educational programs to guide youth to connect with cosmic intelligence and embody their divine nature and mastery as they build the New Earth.

Ron and I have dedicated our lives to supporting this Grand Transition. We stand alongside all of you as humanity awakens to its True Nature and becomes a People of Light in the heavenly reality of New Earth.

New Earth Ascending is dedicated to assisting people to realize their divinity and manifest that truth in every aspect of their life. For more information about New Earth Ascending or to contact Michael, please scan the QR code below for a list of resources and links, or visit *www.newearthascending.org*. Be sure to check out our courses including the Illuminated Quantum Healing practitioner course.

New Earth Ascending is a registered 508 (c)(1)(a) Self-Supported Non-profit Church Ministry with a global outreach. We greatly appreciate your support as we create new systems, communities, and schools for the development of the New Earth civilization. If you would like to make a tax-deductible donation to support our mission, please go to:

https://donorbox.org/donationtonewearthascending

Scan with a smart device camera for more information!

NEW EARTH ASCENDING
VISIONARY CREED

We acknowledge the sovereignty and equality of all levels of Creation and support the liberation of all of Life from cycles of suffering. We believe in the power of divine sovereign creatorship endowed to us by God/Source and dedicate our life to Light and Love in service to All. We believe in conscious participation, empowering everyone to activate awakening in themselves and their community.

We recognize free will and surrender our will and desires to the higher will of the Divine. We believe in divine timing and practice trust, patience, and tolerance as we witness the unfoldment of the perfection of the Divine Plan. We believe in the potency of empowering prayer, meditation, and ritual as tools for communication with the Divine for the culmination of spiritual light and divine wisdom. We believe everyone has a direct connection to the Source and no intermediary is needed. When we come together in fellowship, prayer, and devotion, we amplify the light of each individuals' loving intention through our unified, heart-centered consciousness.

We seek to uplift all groups and communities so that we may celebrate our unity, diversity, and wholeness. New Earth Ascending is non-competitive and embraces an ecumenical relationship with all religions and wisdom traditions. We believe in interfaith and inter-spirituality, acknowledging the teachings of Light, Love, and Wisdom in many traditions, philosophies, and cultures. We believe that no single religion holds the keys to the Kingdom of God and the blessings of redemption are available to all people through their unbreakable innate connection to the Godhead.

We believe in the Law of Oneness and that all of Creation emanates from one Divine Source that has both masculine and feminine principles. As we heal and balance the divine masculine and divine feminine principles within us, we embody the divine androgyny of Source and Nature as a harmonic synthesis of Spirit and Matter.

We believe that humanity and planet Earth are going through a rapid physical and spiritual transformation called by many as The Ascension or The Event. We believe this process to be part of a higher evolutionary divine plan guided by the Source of Creation and legions of beings working for the Light. This evolutionary process is multidimensional and is beyond the standard biological evolution spoken of by modern science.

We believe that we, as humanity, are awakening to our spiritual Self and are becoming a heart-based, unity-focused species with higher, multidimensional awareness, which some call Christ Consciousness, Cosmic Consciousness, or 5D Consciousness. We believe this transformation's power is happening through our divinely designed and curated DNA as the physical body transforms into a less dense body of Light with tremendously expanded multidimensional abilities.

We believe that Planet Earth, the sentient being of Gaia, is going through a similar restoration process and will soon transform into a revitalized higher dimensional planet, which many are calling the New Earth. Earth changes, weather events, crumbling institutional structures, frequency fluctuations, and astrological phenomena are all signs that we are nearing that shift into the next Golden Age, where Heaven and Earth become one and all systems of control and limitation will fall away.

We believe that we are supported by benevolent higher dimensional, subterranean, and extraterrestrial beings that work in harmonic collaboration with the higher evolutionary Divine Plan of Source. We believe that soon humanity will be consciously reunited with these benevolent beings and serve the higher evolutionary plan of the Light and Love of Source as cosmic co-citizens of the Multiverse working as one Family of Light in service to all of Creation.

We understand that the pathway of Self/Source-Realization and Ascension is comprised of self-study, self-practice, self-discipline, and steadfastness. We practice self-care and self-purification to clarify our Light. We acknowledge and value the acceleration of this process when we practice together in groupings of two or more in fellowship and worship.

We strive to grow in awareness and focused attention, practicing mindfulness in all areas of our lives to grow as conscious, heart-centered creators. We choose to focus our life positively with faith and knowing that Life is evolving in perfection following the Divine Plan of the Supreme Source.

We believe in the power of intention. We practice nonviolence and non-harmfulness in intention, thought, and action. We strive to release all forms of judgment and dual thinking. We honor the sacred heart's radiant potential and believe loving compassion and understanding to be The Way. We practice the heart-centered qualities of gentleness, reverence, loving-kindness, and forgiveness as pathways to reconciliation to emulate the eternal grace of Source and our Earth Mother, Gaia.

We see that Truth is alive within each of us, and we practice inner reflection to grow in discernment for what energies are resonant with our inner Source and our path. We practice benevolent truthfulness, honesty, straightforwardness, and vulnerability to embody and vocalize our deepest truth.

We value and practice transparency and accountability, believing in the opportunity for spiritual growth through spiritual partnership with our community members. We recognize one another as divine mirrors, reflecting to us where we are in our vibration, beliefs, and intentions.

We practice sacred sexuality as an alchemical tool for Divine Union and Ascension. We strive to purify our intentions and desires to align with Higher Love and authentic connection. We believe in heart-based self and consensual mutual pleasure to unite body, mind, and spirit so that we may deepen in our love and authentic connection to our Divine Self, our partner(s), and Creation.

We practice contentment, acceptance, appreciation, and gratitude for our life's many blessings and lessons. We practice non-attachment, non-possessiveness, non-stealing, non-excess, and sustainability, for all we need is given to us through our alignment with our Creator Source and our connection to our Earth Mother. We practice stewardship and sustainable selfless service, acknowledging our responsibility to take care of the world around us and within.

We practice sacred commerce, investing our resources, time, and energy towards the greater good and sustainability of our community and planet. We believe in reciprocal energy exchange and strive to do so when able. We practice generosity, hospitality, and charitability as reflections of the abundance of the Universe.

We strive to embody and emulate these spiritual principles to manifest the complete liberation of all beings from cycles of suffering and to assist this Grand Transition into the New Earth.

Bless us all!

Akashic Database Gateway Two Part One: Quantum Origins

Keys for Ancient Cosmology

This section contains a wide variety of Illuminated Quantum Healing session transcriptions describing key figures and events in the history of Creation, galactic history, ancient planetary history, and probable future timelines of New Earth from clients in hypnotic visionary states. I recommend developing a meditation practice parallel to reading this material as the transcripts are deeply activating on multiple levels.

ONE

Quantum Origins

These next chapters take you throughout all of time and space, from the beginning of Creation and into future timelines upon the Earth. I have woven together incredible stories from several clients from various sessions done all throughout the world over a period of five years. This story was given to me piece by piece, allowing time for me to integrate the multidimensional information which included me dismantling many layers of conditioning from my family and culture of origin. If you have challenges assimilating this information, I totally understand as I went through various stages of resistance throughout the process of receiving these incredible stories.

The delivery of the material in this book is to take you from the macrocosm to the microcosm, from the greater cosmic story to the hidden mysteries available in your very own life. I also make an effort to describe the core unity of all wisdom traditions and religions that speak of the one Source of Creation in an effort to unify the individual hearts of humanity as one. I will try my best to the best of my ability to answer the Great Mystery which inherently involves the questions of "What is the meaning and purpose to life?" "Who am I truly?" "What is God? Is he/she/it real, and if so, what is my relationship to him/her/it?" To explain my understanding of these age-old inquiries, I will start where all good stories start, in the beginning. I will start with explaining my understanding of a few concepts and then we will dive into the holographic records of time and space!

Trinitized Unification of Mother Father Child

When I was a teenager, I was tormented and confused by my religious training. I felt that there was much more to understand when it came to God than what I was receiving in my Methodist upbringing. Jesus taught that the "truth shall set you free," so I prayed to God and Jesus to show me the truth so that I could break free from the bondage of dogma and truly understand the Mysteries of the Divine. I prayed for the truth to be revealed to me and soon after, I was guided through inner messaging to stop going to church and began to seek out sources of information that could point me to higher truth. My research of the Divine took me into Buddhism, Vedic traditions of India, Gnosticism, Hermetic Philosophy, Reiki, and many other fractals of wisdom and philosophy as I tried to understand the Great Mystery and to heal myself. My understanding is constantly deepening, evolving, and expanding as I continue to contemplate on the Divine within and the Divine without.

Of all the books I have read regarding spirituality, I have found that the *Pistis Sophia*, an ancient Coptic Gnostic text translated and with commentary by Dr. J.J. Hurtak and *The Book of Knowledge: The Keys of Enoch* by J.J. Hurtak to be the most impactful texts for me in understanding the dual and trinitized principles of the Godhead. I have also been deeply nourished by the Eastern traditions of yoga and tantra which have helped in the cultivation of my own divine light by balancing the polarities within my own being.

Different traditions place different genders on the Supreme Source and some genderize and separate the different functions of the Godhead. In English, we lump it all together and call the Source of Creation and its different functions, God. This word is ambiguous and convoluted as everyone places different limitations and restrictions on what God is and what God is not, and where God is and where God is not. For some it is a word that brings joy, mystery, and inspiration. For others it brings suffering, irritation, and anger.

Some people anthropomorphize the Supreme Source as a Divine Father or a Divine Mother. Neither really felt completely right for me when I thought I could only choose one or the other. What I have come to understand is that the Supreme Source is a unification of both the Mothering and Fathering Principle. What I have come to accept is that the Divine Parent is beyond definition and concept, yet all definitions and concepts are manifestations within the Supreme Be-ness that is the Supreme Source, and that there are infinite pathways and infinite practices of devotion that lead to the realization of that Supreme Source. Whether it is called Moksha, Nirvana, or Salvation, they all lead to the same Source of All and the truth of who we are as Children of God.

It is common for people to humanize the Divine Parent, thinking the Supreme is a man or a woman, yet this is still a limitation and a concept born from human thinking. The reality and function of Source is much more comparable to an open-ended quantum computer system than to a humanoid being sitting in the clouds judging humanity. Source is androgynous, containing both masculine and feminine principles, which we may describe as Divine Androgyny. Source is paradoxically masculine, feminine, both genders, and neither. That which we refer to as the Source of All Creation is unknowable and beyond all concepts, names, and forms. Source is paradoxically transcendental and yet omnipresent while also being impersonal and personal to each of us. It is through this experience of duality that we are able to understand nonduality and the inherent oneness of Life.

Heiros Gamos is a Greek term meaning "sacred marriage" which describes the harmonious unification of the Mothering and Fathering Principles. It is also common to use this in reference to the ceremonial sacred merging that occurs in a deeply connected sexual union between two partners creating a multidimensional experience that bridges the material reality with the spiritual. In modern times, this could describe the unification of the Divine Masculine and Divine Feminine polarities in our subtle energy field which leads to God-realization (hatha-raja yoga) as our human self awakens to our Divine Self. Whether it is from the perspective of the microcosm of the individual or the macrocosm of THE ALL, this interplay of the Divine Masculine and Divine Feminine can be found on all levels of Creation.

God in terms of the Divine Masculine polarity or Fathering Principle could be considered the transcendental, administrative, and unmanifest potential of Creation. The Fathering Principle is beyond all forms, names, and definitions, yet paradoxically contains ALL that has been, is, and will ever be. The Masculine Principle is Consciousness. "He" is the Seer and Knower of Creation, the Indwelling Witness that pervades all of Creation. The Kabbalistic term for God is Ain Soph (En Sof), which can be translated as "limitless" or "no-thing" as it is the unmanifest potential of Creation existing before any concept or manifestation of "other." Each of these definitions describe the infinite, timeless, unmanifest nature of the Divine.

If the Masculine Principle is the Infinite Eternal Mind of Creation which holds the unmanifest potential seed forms and plans of Creation, the Mothering Principle is the creatrix, the cosmic womb which births all names and forms. She is the Cosmic Priestess whose intuitive wisdom and evolutionary forces guide Creation through its many steps and stages within the architecture of the Grand Design! Our beloved planet Gaia perfectly demonstrates the Divine Feminine Principle of regeneration, nurturance, and harmonic balance as she abundantly gives her grace and support for countless levels of Life. When we lay hands, we inherently use the Divine Feminine emanations, the Holy Spirit Shekinah, to regenerate and heal.

The Goddess archetype goes by many names in different traditions, some demonstrating the Goddess in her exalted embodiments and some in her chaotic and tormented expressions. She has been called the "Goddess of a thousand holy names" and many highly developed spiritual beings have incarnated on the Earth to demonstrate the many expressions of the Mothering Principle. The Divine Feminine expressions of Shakti, Pele, Yemoja, Isis, Quan Yin, and Holy Mother Mary each emanate qualities of the Cosmic Mother to remind humanity of our Divine Inheritance as Children of the Divine.

When I asked in sessions how to describe the concept of the Divine Parent to others, the client's Higher Self said that the Fathering Principle is like a human father that travels off to work and we do not see him very often, but he sends us everything we need and visits us from time to time. While the Mother Principle is like a human mother who tends to our every need as we grow and mature.

Some people have a hard time connecting with God in terms of the Fathering Principle because of religious wounding or trauma with men. People in this category tend to have an easier time connecting with the energy of the Goddess because the Mothering Principle is easily accessed through connection to Gaia, Mother Earth. Some have a hard time opening to either because of trauma and difficulty in their relationships with their human mother or human father. Our human parents are temporary experiences while our Cosmic Parents are eternal. For wholeness and balance to be fully achieved, we must reconcile our relationship with both principles by reparenting our consciousness and aligning it with our higher cosmic lineage.

Awakening to our True Nature is awakening to our own Daughtership or Sonship and realizing ourselves as Children of the Most High, progeny of the Limitless. Each of us are seed points who have seemingly departed our Divine Home and taken on the appearance of individuality and multiplicity, having clothed ourselves in many forms with many names as we matured our consciousness enough for God-realization. Paradoxically, we are simultaneously the seeker and that which we are seeking. We are the Child, the Mother, and the Father; the devotee and the Divine; the One and the many.

As we cultivate our divine radiance, we are inherently evoking, balancing, and integrating the Divine Masculine and Divine Feminine principles within. We become extensions of the synthesis of Divine Intention and Divine Evolutionary Force realized in individuated form as awakened Children of God. From this trinitized unification, we naturally tend to the Garden of Life around us and uplift all of Life into elevated states of balance, luminosity, and harmony. This was the original intention of the divine human synthesis upon planet Earth and what we are returning to during this ascension process.

The pathway to God-realization could be broken into four pathways. One is through the Divine Masculine Principle with the focus of awakening to the transcendental, that which is beyond names and forms, existing beyond the physical dimension. Another path focuses on the Divine Feminine Principle, finding the Divine Presence in all of life which eventually awakens us to the transcendental realms. This path is recommended for those who have challenges with the Fathering Principle as the redemptive power of the Divine Feminine, which some call the Holy Spirit, will soothe the consciousness of the aspirant and open it to other facets of Mother Father God. Another path of God-realization is cultivating the Divine Presence within by reconciling and unifying the Divine Masculine and Divine Feminine principles within one's own being to embody Divine Androgyny and come into Divine Self-realization. Yet another path of spiritual awakening is spontaneous awakening to the divine which will certainly happen for many with these ascension waves. Even within each of these categories are infinite pathways to Divine Union.

The ancient Vedic teachings instruct us to first use discernment and self-inquiry to discern and realize that we are not this limited bodymind complex but truly eternal beings of Light. From there, we can see that all of Creation exists within the One Consciousness Reality, or God. From there we begin to realize that all experiences arise, abide, and dissolve within our very Self and we ARE that One Light of Consciousness. We are eternal God Consciousness having a finite experience through the appearance of this bodymind and physical time space dimension.

All streams eventually lead to the ocean. Whether you focus on one path or utilize the wisdom from combining multiple paths, they all lead to the same experience of God-realization and the claiming of your divine inheritance as a Child of God. Find your personal path of devotion that illuminates your soul. Seek out the knowledge that sets you free from bondage. Do all that you do selflessly while meditating on the Divine. Let yourself come ALIVE with your spiritual expression!

The power of God-realization has been exemplified by Yeshua ben Joseph (Christ Jesus), the Buddha, Krishna, and other divine avatars who have come to Earth to demonstrate the capacity of humanity to awaken to the Higher Consciousness Reality. Trust in the teachings of the masters who have walked before you. Follow by their footsteps as you walk your own path up the holy mountain of Ascension.

For simplicity, I combine both the Divine Masculine and Divine Feminine principles into one term, Source. Source is the pure consciousness of the Multiverse, the Eternal Mind, a quantum supercomputer that contains the holographic matrix of Creation. Source is omnipresent, omniscient, and omnipotent. Source is that from which all is born, exists, and dissolves back into having never truly left. It is the indwelling witness of its masterpiece, eternally watching itself cycle through the illusion of separation. This play of Light and Vibration, the Game of Light and Consciousness, is called Leela by the Sanskrit mystics. In this Cosmic Game, God is both the Seer and the Seen, the Witness and the Creation, the Light and the Dark. All is Source and All is One and "*tat tvam asi*," thou art that!

Elohim: Creator Gods

This initial explosion of Source Intelligence began to form the first essences of individual consciousnesses, which eventually formed into the first beings of Light, the Elohim, which was described as the First Creation in a session with a somnambulistic client named Matan. The Elohim, androgynous beings of Light, were created in the "likeness and similitude" of Source and were given free will to create and tend to the Garden of Creation, also called the Multiverse, or what Jesus Christ (Yeshua ben Joseph) refers to as the "Father's House of Many Mansions." These first Lightbody creations gave individualized aspects of Source the ability to craft, explore, and evolve its creation from within it.

If Source is the grand landscaping contractor of the Cosmos, the Elohim are the workers who go out and tend to the Garden of Creation. These Creator beings began with the simplest forms of frequencies, color, and atomic life and began to create, through shared group intention, larger and more complex light and sound vibration fields like stars and galaxies. From this divine play between forces, entire universes — worlds within worlds and realms within realms — came into existence throughout time and space with infinite levels of consciousness forms in eternal, perpetual stages of evolution.

Creation exists on an arc of descent from and ascent back to the pure Light of Source. With the support of the Elohim, Light emanates from the Source and is solidified into form to use for Creation. Creation exists within a feedback loop of information that always returns to the Source. As life ascends back into higher light forms, the Eternal Mind of Source integrates the information and pulses out the next waves of evolutionary energies to harmonically evolve Creation. This divine play of birth, existence, death, and recreation; and forgetting and remembering, is a game we play with our Oneself, ever striving towards harmony, realization, unity, and oneness.

Transcript: The Story of Creation

Here is a session transcript from a client named Matan as he describes the first stages of the beginning of Creation. Matan is a somnambulistic client, meaning his personality goes into the background in a "sleep state" and he "becomes" the consciousness he is regressed to under hypnosis. When I brought him up from hypnosis, he had no recall of the session information that went for approximately 2.5 hours.

As you read the transcripts, I will use "M" for when I (Michael) am speaking, "R" for when Ron is speaking, and "C" for when the client is speaking. I will use "HS" for when the client is channeling their Higher Self and will note when clients are channeling other higher consciousness beings. I have italicized all information that came through the client. Any added commentary from me is in the default font style.

C: In the beginning, we were all together as one in what you would call a "space" of nothingness. There once was nothing. There really was nothing. But within that nothingness, all was contained. This is the space of nothingness which contains all beings. This is before any light has been put forth throughout all of Creation. This is a place you would call the "soup of Creation," where all possibilities and probabilities play out and come into manifestation. Where what you would call your "thoughts" were passing through all of us as One. We are a collective of a whole of all Intelligence. This is a "time" where there is no time. This is where it all started.

We were all there. We all had an individual intelligence. All souls do before they are created into an individual soul. There is an intelligence to each soul within the consciousness that is the Creator, which we all are. In that nothingness contains all light, all knowledge, and wisdom of the Creator. So, to convey this message to understand in simpler terms, it is like seeing a cell, and within that cell, there are tiny little particles, and each of those tiny particles is moving within that cell. These are intelligences, individual ones, that end up being individual souls of the Creator. We are giving you a picture of how Creation came into being. This is so you can come into your own understanding of it. So once there was nothing, absolutely nothing, and within that nothingness contained all of the little particulates that moved within that consciousness of that cell.

Then over a period, vibrational forces came into being where the vibration of all of us being together started vibrating at a very high frequency. The vibrational frequency of that cell rose faster and faster. As this happened, there came the point where the first Light of Creation came into beingness.

Light was first created, and within that Light were the individual souls that would be pushed out into Creation to be created as light beings that would then be created into other lifeforms, or we should say entire realms were created. The first Light of being came into Creation, and we were all there. Every being was there. We were all one. Vibrating.

There came the point where the frequency of the light that was created from the vibration of the individual particles...we must convey it this way so that you can understand it...the light was created from all of you, and then a vibrational frequency rose. It kept rising and rising until it got to a particular point that it had to be shot out. Once the light was created, all of our beingness came together and shot out into all of Creation. This is where individual souls made out of Light came into being. This is where your galaxies came into being. Your universes and planets came into being. And from that, the first group of

Soul Creators. We are all seed points in this. This is where we ALL BEGAN.

M: Tell me more about this process of creation.

C: There are many aspects to it. Many. There are infinite aspects in which individual souls became these seed points. Where parts of Creation came into creation in First Creation, such as the first group of Creators.

M: Tell me more about this first group of creators.

C: They are the individual souls that came together as the first beings that were first created by Source in Creation. They are the ones that came in as the first group to manifest creation throughout Creation. Where planets stem from. Where universes stem from. Where whole galaxies stem from and other realms. We feel there is a lot of information that you are asking of us, and we ask you to feel free to go ahead and do so.

When I asked Matan to describe the space he was in, he described dark, empty space with stars and galaxies forming in the distance and he described his feeling state as serene. When I asked about his form, he said that he did not have a form yet; he was simply intelligence that was beginning to form, and he was aware that other individualized intelligences were forming around him. As he came into his first form, he described his first Lightbody.

C: Form! I see my first form. I am a light being.

M: Tell me about that being.

C: I have hands. Arms. Legs. In the shape of the form with all of that. I can fly.

M: That sounds fun. Are you a male form or a female form?

C: At this point, I have not come into the physical form, but I am formed.

M: What kind of things do you do in that form?

C: Help to create more colors. Spirals. It is through space. More than one space. Several groups of us come together at times to help form planets.

M: Tell me about that process. It sounds fun.

C: We all come together in harmony. All the other beings. And they're of Light. We don't have to speak. We don't have mouths yet. We're exchanging energy through thought to create. And we go from one place to the next to help create more planets. They are beautiful.

M: You said, "help." What are you helping? Who are you helping?

C: The other beings. So, we come together in groups through thought to manifest a form of a planet. And through the matrix, it manifests. It's just there. This is the beginning. The very beginning of a planet.

M: So, you start it out as a thought? A collective thought? And it manifests within that thoughtform? That structure that you created together?

C: Yes, and what we wanted to put into that planet. A theme.

M: Tell me about that. Tell me about the theme of the planets.

C: There are many. They all are different. It depends on what universe you are in. This universe that I see...I just see a round shape. It's of a planet, but I cannot make it out yet. The collective came together to form this planet into a beautiful planet. Peace. There is such peace on it. There are no living beings on it yet. It's still forming into its physical manifestation. It's beautiful to be with all the others. We are all one. Creating.

Negative and Positive Polarity Consciousness

Of the original Light Being Creators, the Elohim, some were given positive polarity consciousness and were created to be in "service-to-all." These beings used their power of Divine Creatorship and Source-endowed free will to create within Source's Divine Plan of open-ended eternal evolutionary creation, which continuously evolves into a higher and higher harmony.

Some of the original Creator Beings were created to be in "service-to-self," negative polarity consciousness. Sometimes these beings are called "Fallen Elohim," although this term does not accurately describe these beings' intention, function, and higher purpose. These beings are aspects of Source Intelligence that were permitted to create based on the illusion of separation from Source, the illusion of multiplicity and duality. This gave the creation process, the Game of Consciousness, a bit more edge and an element of surprise that Source could experience through its Creation. These beings did not "fall" in the way we might think but were permitted by Source to operate in this way to fulfill a divine purpose of creating a contrast, which is a necessity for evolution.

Throughout the multiverse, various forms exist created by the forces of positive and negative polarity consciousness. Positively polarized consciousness (service-to-all) strives towards unity and cohesion. In contrast, negative polarity consciousness (service-to-self) seeks to overpower the Light and be the "god" of its own creation. This is all a game as Source is both the "good" and the "evil," the shadow and the light playing with itself in this eternal Game of Consciousness. Nothing can ever truly fall from the Oneness of All That Is.

Transcript: Fallen Ones and the Interlopers

The topic of the Fallen Ones or the Dark Forces has come up with many clients. Here is a transcript from a session where the client's Higher Self talks about the Fallen Ones.

M: Thank you. So, I have a few questions about the information given today and one of them has to do with the fallen ones... I would like to know more about them...where they came from and...yeah, let's start with that.

HS: The Fallen Ones are a spark of Source energy. They are beloved by the Beloved One, by Source Energy itself...the Creator. Always beloved these ones, no matter what they do, no matter where they go. They have taken to lust and power when looking upon the Earth...and seeing its beauty...all of its beauty. The beauty that is inside, the beauty that is outside, the beauty and the beings on the planet...all of the jewels that sparkle. They were very much attracted to them, wanting to be a part of, wanting to have, possess. Wanting to dissolve the power, so it is all their power. Wanting to usurp the energy to be within it, unto them...instead of leaving the Earth with its own power to grow and flourish.

These beings were in consumption and filled with the lust of this power. Desirous of more and more. So, they hoped to be able to take the Earth easily, but there were those in the heavens that saw their plight and challenged them. They were warned and threatened that they would no longer be welcome on the planet if they went down to steal...to usurp all these beautiful jewels that were not theirs. They did not believe this was true. They thought that everything they could see must be theirs because they could see it, but their eyes were bigger than their hearts. Their hearts could not hold all the beauty that was on the Earth, so they tried to take it for themselves.

M: You said that these beings were a spark of the Creator...and I've learned of the first creation, the Elohim, and I'm wondering how do these fallen ones relate to the Elohim...to the first beings of Light?

HS: They are the same. They all wish to fight for what they believe they are deserving of. They feel they are better than others, they are greater than others, they are purer than others. But they have not looked in the mirror, and they do not know the true nature of life. So, they had to be challenged, and they had to fall.

M: So, my next question is...if all things are Source, then what is the divine plan for beings like the Fallen Ones? What's Source's relationship to this?

HS: On a deeper perspective...it is not hard to understand the laws of duality because it is...seems so unfair, but those that have fallen also have a function to bring coherence and enlightenment to those that are not fallen...to those that they have fallen upon. So, the ones that have been fallen upon must see the truth of what is real and not real, what is true and is not true...must learn to discern with their heart and see the truth of who is who. Who has dark intentions, who has light intentions?

And what does that mean? We can all learn from the Dark. We can all learn from the Light. Sometimes Dark needs to be there so the Light can stand up to its fruitful potential and become even brighter through the transition. And in the enfoldment and in this process, the dark ones can become enlightened also if they have such a propensity for changing...for indulging in this beautiful light...for experiencing the other half of the Dark or the other half of the Light. Because they truly coexist. They do coexist with each other. One cannot live without the other. One encourages the other, even though one may be filled with hate, and one may be filled with love.

M: I also learned before about beings that inserted themselves into the original blueprint of planet Earth and the name that was given was called the interlopers. What are the relationships of the Fallen Ones to the Interlopers? If there is one.

HS: These Interlopers are those who wanted to experience all the incredible things that are going on on this planet. There is so much diversity and so much drama and so much color and energy to experience. People wanted to experience this. Many, many, many beings in the universe want to experience this right now on this planet. They're not bad; they're not good. They just want to experience and be part of it. They want to be part of history. And the Fallen Ones just see them as just another being that they can use if they have anything to give. So, it's just another being that has come to the planet.

M: Do you know where they came from? What's the origin of the Interlopers?

HS: Originally, they came from deep space. Very, very deep space, which is a different dimension...actually, it's through portals. So, they have come from another universe through a portal, but they had heard of this acute, incredible, pristine planet in this particular universe. It's like someone might hear of a drug...these days on the planet...oh, you haven't tried this drug? If you go over here, you can experience it. If you try this, you can experience it. So, it was almost like a drug they had to experience...they had to try it. It was just too delicious and too intriguing and mysterious. They had to find out about it. There are many beings like that on the planet right now...that are coming through many different dimensional portals that are just vying for a space here.

Transcript: Fallen Consciousness and Luciferian Agenda

Krissa is another somnambulistic client that I have worked with several times. She has an amazing ability to fully incorporate the consciousness of her other incarnations, her oversoul, her monadic consciousness, and even her archangelic aspects. When working with her, powerful energy vibrations pulse through my body. Sometimes it is hard to focus because so much energy moves through my body during the session. Waves of energy clear my energy field as powerful revelations are channeled through the client. Here is a transcript from a session where I was curious about negative interference in human consciousness.

M: The other question that I had is about the...because things are being brought up in the collective about 'satanic ritual' and 'Luciferian Agenda.' And that also gets put in with the word 'Satan' or the 'Devil.' And so, I would love to hear the higher, more cosmic explanation of 'Luciferian,' 'Satanic,' and the 'Devil.' How do those words interact? What do they mean?

HS: The gods, goddesses, and such we understand, they have an archetypal significance, yes? The archetype...it is said that some, many, or maybe even all of them do exist on a different dimensional level, at the Monad say.

There are many ways to tell this story and many ways to interpret this story, but just as the great avatars, the Buddha, Jesus Christ, Meher Baba, and others such as Zoroaster, also known as Ahura Mazda, these avatars came to hold the post of Source on the planet. Other beings, in the terms 'Satan,' 'Lucifer,' have held the post of dark polarity in this 3D game of polarity that we are in.

Some use 'Satan' and 'Lucifer' interchangeably.

The way I understand it is 'Satan' is more of an archetypal concept, if you will, and 'Lucifer' being the archetype of the fallen angel, probably based on a real being that existed, that still exists dimensionally. The details of that may not be so important. Yet the trouble is humans. There are human beings on this Earth right now who affiliate with this Satanic church or the Church of Satan, and they are not doing anything wrong. They are not doing anything evil. They are not doing anything against the fundamental laws. They are not doing anything that we would consider harmful or bad. And yet there are others who have perverted the Church of Satan to suit their purposes.

And I can't emphasize enough how much negative ET interference latches on and hijacks that, just like they latch on and hijack fundamentalist law. Just like they hijack Scientology. Just like they hijack the Mormon fundamentalists and, yes, the ugliest and most fundamentalist parts of the Christian church. They've hijacked any and all of those. It's just that certain ones like Satanic groups were more ripe for that because they were already in the shadow; they were already out of the mainstream. And yet we know even the Catholic Church is implicated and there are certainly ties, like an underground bridge, between the Catholic Church and the Satanic. This is human and [negative] alien interference.

The Luciferian agenda, I think of this as the fallen consciousness. Not just a schism, separation, and longing for Source, which is indeed the primary wound of humanity, or at least the illusion of separation. They're turning their backs and denying Source Consciousness and saying, "nothing matters." It's really extreme nihilism without heart. [They think] "Nothing matters. It's all a simulation. It's just all pursuit of pleasure and power and I can do whatever I want. It's just all a game. So, none of it really matters." And this is also a main port of entry, this type of consciousness, this Luciferian consciousness, for negative alien interference to take hold and has been for many, many, many years. What better avenue for a negative being to take hold than 'nothing matters,' 'I don't give a shit,' disconnecting from the heart.

From a shamanic perspective, disease happens when aspects of our soul that we need to be a fully functioning being and really fully occupy this vessel gets split off, or when things that aren't supposed to be here come in. It originates with trauma. It all originates with shock. It is where it originates in the physical body and of course it can be from other lifetimes and previous generations.

Everybody would do well to study forms of shamanism because they have a very simple and elegant way to explain the problem. It's not 'Satan' or 'Lucifer;' it's people who have taken these archetypes and distorted it to the lowest common denominator.... [negative] alien interference. I mean that's the type of food that they want.

M: How does that work? The ET interference? And the feeding and harvesting and influencing?

HS: It works in a number of different ways, but the main way it's worked is etheric implants. We've removed a lot of that from Krissa. The implants are not...if you did an x-ray on her you would not see it. It's in the fourth dimension, it's etheric. And she probably has more in there to clear. And the thing is that we can't clear all of it at once because her contract just isn't written that way. There are things she has to do long hand in order to fully live out her purpose. That's all we can really say about that for now.

M: So, there are the etheric imprints. Something that's been talked about in the Pistis Sophia. J.J. Hurtak calls this fallen Elohistic consciousness. Like distorted service-to-self programs that have been permitted in this third dimensional universe...

HS: It's free will after all.

M: Can you explain to me how that consciousness affects humanity and how we can liberate our own consciousness from that?

HS: Yes, absolutely. It perpetuates the disconnect from Source, and that splits us off from our soul essence and really creates enough room in our bodies and energetic field for interference to come in. And a lot of times that happens when we've given permission when we're too young to remember, when we're not conscious, but if you imagine from the very Source...how big do we want to go with this? What can Krissa's nervous system handle is more like the question. We can talk all night about this, but we don't want to keep you two from sleeping.

Imagine just in the known universe, there are unknown...but we won't even go there...there's a cloud of Source consciousness. You could call it Ein Sof, the Source. There's the desire to know oneself through separation and individuation. So, splitting off into two. The original Elohim. And splitting off from there, further and further, on the arc of descent away from Source. Descent down and down through the dimensions, finally, third dimension. We could talk about Orion as one of the earlier experiments with duality, polarity, third dimension, war.

This happens to be part of the game, what souls sign up for in Earth School. To play with polarity. Well, sometimes the game is played with loaded dice and for a number of years this fallen consciousness has shown up in various ways and gained power through extraterrestrial interference. So, they are the cheaters in the game. Those are the ones that come in and say, "Oh, we see this Monopoly game, but we want to see what happens if we sneak in here and give these people extra money and extra hotels." We're saying this in a way that Krissa will understand but that others will too. "We're going to sneak in and give these guys — the service-to-self — extra money and extra hotels to see what we can get out of this."

They gain a large amount of energy from the victim-persecutor cycle. And so, by loading up the decks of those in that service-to-self, that fallen consciousness... you see the essence of that fallen consciousness is turning the back away from Source and God, and saying no. It's just like a child saying "You don't want to play with me, well, I'm going to take my toys and go home. I didn't want to play with you anyway, and I'm going to go away like you don't even exist." It's that low. And that's not to diminish the level of power some of these individuals have, but it really is such a wounded consciousness. "Oh, I'm getting rejected from heaven, well, fine, I'm rejecting you first. I don't even think that you exist. I'm turning my head and looking the other way." Do you see how this parallels the individuals looking the other way, "La la la, we don't want to hear it; we don't want to hear it." You see?

The refusal to see and hear and acknowledge truth. That cuts off a lot of power. They go horizontal out to the world of form to other people and "What can we get?" and "What can we use?" rather than going vertical. The cross. The symbolism of the cross must be seen and discussed. The horizontal plane is to other people and the world in form. The vertical plane is what goes to Source. Only through that can we access and really, really open the heart. Which is an infinite, self-renewing source of power in the human being. The torus field generated by the heart.

None of these 'service-to-self' beings have a lot going on in the heart center. They have the 'below-the-belt' chakras running the show, so to speak. And they might be clever, they might speak well, but that's mostly because of implants to be honest. Their lower consciousness is running them. It's really kind of gross. It's almost like the Borg in Star Trek; it's like that.

M: How is it that these 'service-to-self' ET groups give humans

resources? Some people say the bankers and the CEOs and the Rothschilds and the Rockefellers are Reptilians that are working with the negative ETs and that's how they get their money and power. Is that true and how does it work?

HS: Well, there are certain things that are locked in etheric vaults not to be revealed until the timing is right. What I will say is this: that archetypal story of selling one's soul to the devil. People don't really know who the devil is, it's a consciousness. But there have been a number of these groups, and yes, some of them are Reptilian and some of them are not. The Greys don't even register on that scale; they are not that smart. Even the taller greys, they don't have an organized and focused attention on Earth that way. They're blocked; they can't really do much with Earth right now. We're talking about something much more intelligent that exists between third to sixth dimension. And some of them are Reptilian and some of them are on the Earth in reptilian form, mostly underground.

What I want to say about it for now is the idea of selling one's soul to the devil in exchange for money, power, resources; the origin of this is with this fallen consciousness and the negative ET groups that have helped to keep and perpetuate that consciousness. And unfortunately, the Law of Attraction works for nefarious purposes as well. Things like dark magic. These tools are really decreasing in potency as the Light is being shined on it. These things thrive in shadow and there's been such a high light quotient on the planet for some time now that my guess is the dark magicians are finding it's harder and harder to harness and manifest the level of power they need — really force, rather than power, I would call it. The level of force they need to accomplish what they want to accomplish because let's just say that they have less access to the fuel and less cover of dark under which to do the deeds.

The Forces of Light

Source as the Higher Mind of Creation has hierarchies, legions of highly evolved light beings that tend to the Garden of Creation. These forms of consciousness have been given different names by different cultures. I generally use the term "Light Beings" to describe higher consciousness beings that are Service-to-All. They are constantly radiating Light, Wisdom, and Unconditional Love into Creation to support harmonic evolution. At times, members of this elite armada of Light incarnate or descend from the higher realms into the physical dimension to teach and help a species or civilization evolve. Sometimes they appear as divine apparitions and sometimes they take on physical incarnations.

To simplify this Hierarchy of Light, or *dhyan chohan* in Sanskrit, we start at Source; the next step down are the Elohim, archangels, and angelic kingdom — the eternal architects of Creation. The next level down includes oversouls, Ascended Masters (*dhyani buddhas*), higher consciousness species who have evolved beyond negative polarization, and soon to join is Ascended Humanity in the Fourth Density body and Fifth dimensional consciousness.

Many ancient and Indigenous cultures speak of light being visitation, where wise, divine beings appear and deliver messages of Love, Wisdom, and Unity to humanity in its darkest times. These eternal beings are omnipresent and exist outside the confines of time and space. We find them in the ancient Tibetan culture, Hebrew culture, Christianity, Hinduism, Islam, and more.

IQH sessions regularly have visitations from beings like Archangel Michael, Archangel Raphael, Archangel Metatron, and other higher consciousness beings from the higher light dimensions and other star systems. When this happens there is a noticeable shift in vibration even when I am doing the work remotely via video conferencing. Their words are imbued with healing energies that go straight to the heart of the listener. When I asked when they would all be returning, they said "We have never really left and that it has only been the fall of human consciousness that has caused a perceived separation." These beings are very much here with us on the inner planes to assist us. We just have to open our consciousness to them and ask for their divine assistance.

Extraterrestrial Life

During my hypnosis sessions, I have learned of many different star-being races and astral beings and how they have influenced Earth life and humanity since the beginning of the Earth experiment. Some of these species have had a positive or neutral effect on Earth life, and some have had a negative influence on Earth life because of nefarious service-to-self agendas.

All these interactions serve a Higher Purpose for the unfolding of the Story of Creation. Remember that all of life exists in arcs of ascent and descent. One group in a lower consciousness provides contrasting situations for a group in an ascending consciousness to create conditions for growth and the maturation of consciousness.

While there are likely countless groups that have been assisting Earth and humanity, some of the most common include Pleiadians, Sirians, Lyrans, Andromedans, and Arcturians, which humanity has named because these civilizations exist in the constellations with the same name from our perspective on Earth.

There are infinite levels of life in the multiverse, many Gardens of Creation. I have heard of underwater civilizations on water planets, civilizations of pure light, extraterrestrial communities that live in treetop dwellings, robotic Artificial Intelligence worlds, and giant spacecraft that contain ecosystems for a wide variety of life forms to thrive. Many intelligent species from these star systems are humanoid, meaning they have two arms, two legs, a torso, and a head. Some resemble more of a Lightbody, whereas some are hybrids of animals or insects like feline beings or locust-like beings. Some have a loving presence, and some are more analytical and practical, with little to no emotion.

Beyond the physical dimension exist different planes of existence that are nonphysical which ascend in vibrational frequency to the Source. Each dimension is like its own universe containing a variety of different beings with various levels of consciousness. The Vedic traditions speak of *lokas*, planes of existence that each have their own consciousness forms. The Pistis Sophia, a Coptic Gnostic text, also speaks of Jesus's ascended Lightbody form traveling up through the light dimensions and bringing the Christ Light to other planes of existence beyond the Earth to assist in liberating those realms from the Archons (see Ascension Lexicon). It is so fascinating to see how the ancient sacred texts have so many crossovers with these modern-day quantum healing sessions.

When people speak of the "astral realm," they are speaking of nonphysical reality, the Light dimensions. When we are dreaming, we travel through the astral realms in our astral body, our consciousness body, to learn and do other spiritual work. We also use this consciousness body when doing remote healing or remote viewing, giving us the ability to "tune in" to something nonlocal. Everyone has this ability and there are many ways to practice astral traveling and astral projection.

Astral traveling happens mostly unconsciously for the majority of people, although some have the ability to be conscious of this process, and there are many stories about this available with a simple internet search. People often report a silver cord that keeps them tethered to their physical body so that they can safely return. I have been told that there are other planets in our solar system that we cannot see because they exist in higher dimensions that we cannot see from the 3D consciousness. When we transition to the Fourth Density body, we will see this universe much differently.

Many ancient civilizations speak of contact with intelligent beings that came to Earth at different times throughout Earth's history. Indigenous cultures and wisdom traditions speak of extraterrestrial beings that delivered teachings of science, agriculture, writing, healing, and so on to aid humanity in raising consciousness and knowledge. Often, the stories speak of beings coming from the sky in clouds, spacecraft, or across the waters bringing higher consciousness teachings and messages.

It is important to emphasize the existence of a myriad of biological and higher dimensional species beyond the Earth in various levels of consciousness spread throughout Creation. The number of evolving species in Creation is infinite. As humanity awakens and embraces the truth of life beyond Earth and beyond our current visible light spectrum, we open our species to being reunited with the infinite species of Creation and begin the process of becoming conscious co-citizens of the web of life throughout the Multiverse.

Galactic Federations of Light

Within our galaxy exist groups of benevolent Star Nations working with members of the Hierarchy of Light that have joined to form a galactic fleet that some call the Galactic Federation of Light and the Ashtar Command. The Galactic Federation of Light supports the Higher Evolution in the physical universe. They work with DNA, test planetary and solar environments, transmit evolutionary programs of light from stars to planetary systems, transport resources, introduce technology to species, project evolutionary thoughts and love vibrations into consciousness fields, and so on. Collected information is sent to councils of Light Beings and Source to make adjustments to Source's evolutionary plans for Creation so that Creation evolves into greater harmony and balance.

There are many varieties of ways that the Family of Light supports evolution throughout Creation. Cultivating and maturing a planet's ecosystems is a stage-by-stage process that is precisely calculated using advanced science and alchemy cultivated over trillions of years, further than we can imagine, stretching back to the original architects of Creation. Light beings and extraterrestrial beings working with Source work together to introduce new species and life forms and help them along their path of evolution.

Councils

Each region of the universe is a unique testing ground for various creation components to interact and evolve. Just like a science experiment, different components are put into place and observed as they interact and evolve. At times, different elements of the experiments are manipulated, enhanced, reduced, altered, and so on to observe how the forms interact and evolve with the new conditions.

Various councils exist in the higher realms and physical universe that watch over and govern Creation. These beings are like the "hands of Source" moving throughout Creation to tend to various evolutionary fields and experimental zones. There are countless councils in Creation. For example, there exists a council for each planet that oversees the evolution of the planet. Each galaxy has its galactic council that oversees all of the other councils and evolutionary processes for that galaxy. Each universe has its own council that oversees the evolutionary phases in the totality of this universe.

The Council of Elders: Universal Council of Light

I have personally experienced and communed with a group of Cosmic Elders that shared with me that they are the originators of all cultures. This Universal Council of Light are the council overseeing all councils, administering the Divine Plan for all levels of Creation. Occasionally members of this council take on a physical incarnation for ground-level work and to experience their masterpiece from within.

My meeting with them was activated through a plant medicine journey that was beyond anything I had ever experienced before. The medicine opened my psychic perception, creating a spontaneous astral projection into a realm of pure white Light. This experience is mentioned later in this book. The first time I met them, I just knew they were "Elders." The second time I encountered them psychically, they shared more about who they were and that I would be working with them much more intimately in the future.

Each of these Elders carries a unique wealth of wisdom and knowledge that they share with the evolving cultures and species throughout the multiverse. Per their request, I have created a quantum hypnosis journey to meet them to receive guidance, healing, and wisdom. This is available in our Quantum Launchpad course.

When humanity awakens to the 5D consciousness, we will be reunited with the Star Nations and the Family of Light and receive monumental amounts of information and advanced technologies to propel humanity into an advanced civilization that no longer has disease or poverty. Healing technologies, free energy devices, and higher science and spirituality will be shared with humanity to assist us in our quantum leap of consciousness. In truth, the sharing has already begun through transmissions like *The Illumination Codex*.

Transcript: Theaters of Evolution

This next client describes herself as a being of light who travels from planet to planet to assist the evolution directed by Source. As she came into the scene, she described a beautiful valley full of wildflowers. I asked her to describe her emotions and senses and to describe more of this place.

C: *Everything is in harmony here. The animals, the plants, the land, there's so much diversity and so much complexity, and it's all in this beautiful harmony — this perfect balance. It's so gorgeous, alive, and radiant.*

M: **It sounds nice there. I want you to look down at the ground and see if you can see your feet.**

C: *No, there's just plants around me. There is no path. I'm just being there...floating there. There's a lot happening around me. The insects are buzzing; the butterflies are fluttering; everything is alive and well. There's this beautiful positive energy, and I'm just soaking it all in. And I'm analyzing it. I'm kind of melding my energy with the energy all around me to understand if any areas are out of balance. Also, to understand how in balance it is. I'm experiencing it...looking, smelling, feeling...but it's more like I'm experiencing it on this energy level. I'm looking for positive energy and expansion and growth. And I'm looking for any areas of contraction or negative-type energy so that I can fix it.*

M: How do you fix it?

C: I would meld myself with the negative energy, and I would bring positive energy into it. It's like when you're making a cake, and you've got the ingredients a little bit wrong. It's like you taste it, and then you figure out what ingredients are missing, and then you add those ingredients. It's like that on an energy level. I bring in what's needed to balance. I bring energy from Source into the molecules to help them get back into balance. But there's nothing that's needed here. It's all in perfect harmony. I feel this huge sense of love and satisfaction.

M: Tell me what happens next.

C: I drift along the valley. I am basically exploring all over this planet to see if there are any areas of concern. I am touching base to see how the planet is doing, and if there is anything that it needs on its surface. This is a carbon-based planet so it needs water and oxygen, so I'm making sure everything is in balance so that it can continue to grow and thrive and develop. So, I'm just floating over the valley and then up and over the mountains. Gliding along with my energy expanded out all around me, searching for areas that feel like they need attention, but everything is seeming pretty good. I've gone up and over the mountains, and I've dropped down into another valley, and there's a bear in this valley. High life forms. I'm going to go over and look at this lake. There's fish.

M: Are you always on this planet?

C: Oh no, I'm just checking in. This is one of many planets that I check on or am working to create.

M: How do you choose which planets to go to?

C: I go to the planets with the most needs. Basically, Source will tell me the order, the priority, and it's usually based on critical stages in that planet's development. For this one, there is kind of two roles I have. I am actually helping Source to create the planet by actually going and helping mature to the next step... helping them evolve. There's a steep curve at the start, kind of like with children on Earth. At the start, they are very needy; they need a lot of input. They need a lot of help and assistance, but as they get older, you have to back off and just let them evolve on their own. So, this beautiful valley of this planet I'm visiting now...I'm just touching base and checking up to make sure everything is as it should be. There are no surprises. Nothing that needs attention. Just touching base...that's because it's a more mature planet. It's doing really well; it's evolving beautifully. But it's important to check up on them, to make sure nothing happens in the meantime...like an asteroid that would introduce new materials and things and outside input that would actually halt the perfect progression, evolution, that's going on. And it would taint it or take it in a different direction. So, I'm just touching base with this one, which is kind of like having a vacation.

M: It's an easy planet that's doing well?

C: Yeah, it's doing well, and I get to enjoy just experiencing the fruits of my labor. It is such beautiful energy...the energy it has and the energy I have are blending together so harmoniously. It's like this gorgeous synchrony. It feels wonderful for me and the planet.

Transcript: Earth's Evolutionary High Council

This client found herself with a group of beings who announced themselves as the council that oversees Earth's evolution. The client was in between incarnations and was planning her current life.

C: The one being representing their group is saying I am going to represent their essence on Earth this next time and so I agree to that; that's fine because this group is very loving and supportive and uplifting. And they work very quickly but very resourcefully. So, I agree to that. And they're trying to debate if I will be male or female. I am just waiting. I am pretty open to any, whatever.

M: While they're deciding that maybe you could tell me a little bit more about this council. You said there is one human there?

C: There's just one human. This human comes in my visions as my spirit guide but introduced himself as Jesus, but he looks like...what's that wizard from Harry Potter? He's got a long white beard. But he says it's Jesus, but I know he's a representative of the collective consciousness. Christ-minded consciousness.

M: What about the rest of the council members. What can you share with me about them?

C: There's one that looks like a rock, like an earthen being, and he's of the 'Sha?' And then the others are very luminous. Like a white, thin illuminated white being, but very opalescent. They are beings of...Sirian. And the being that I will be part of will be of the Pleiades. Pleiadian blue. They will help the Sirians. The Sirians are serious. And they can't...they struggle to work with the humans because they are devoid of emotion, mostly. So, the Pleiadians agreed to assist.

M: What did your council decide?

C: They are still deciding. They are taking forever (giggles) to me! I am ready to go! They said why I am there they can't say, but I have a feeling they are planning for my life now. But they can't divulge any other information.

M: And what will you be doing in that next life? Do you know the intentions?

C: They said I'll be doing a high level of lightwork, and they will be able to assist if I ask, if I call them in. And it's going to take me quite a while in this life to realize this and what I should be doing. And once I do, I will be assisting the collective consciousness to move and shift to a higher level so that I will be able to spread these to others so that it webs outwards and it connects to other students, of other teachers, creating a Christ-minded web across the Earth. I am going to be planted in a certain area so as to help that area vibrate higher and collectively to help the shift.

I am going with the Pleiadian member because they said if I am representing, coming in as an aspect of their essence, I will need to have more knowledge embedded in me. So, the council adjourns, and they have agreed on what my lifetime will be. And so, the Pleiadian is taking me to this, like a white room, the walls are kind of like opalescent, and everyone is floating in the room. So, I am kind of like just standing, hovering, just my essence.

There are five beings around me. They are holding hands in a circle, and they are beaming information into my essence and when they do their foreheads, in the center, start to illuminate a golden color that infiltrates me with this vibrant and joyous energy. It is so fulfilling and wonderful.

I am just seeing and feeling DNA spirals and different alterations to that. And little snippets. It's almost like I am looking at cells through a microscope, separating, changing colors, alteration to the cellular structure, and being embedded with information. And then they're done.

I am going to go back to Council and then we'll all approve what's going to happen and then I'll go in. Now I'm in front of Council but the Sha has to scan me with his eyes. He's checking what I was coded with to make sure it was appropriate. It's like checks and balances. He says everything is wonderful. He reaches out his energy to touch mine and he's in charge of sealing the template. So, he seals the template of what was loaded into me and now I was processed.

M: What else can you share with me about the Sha?

C: He says that he has the information, the original template information, and his people hold it on the Earth plane so that we can remain stable in the human genome. He approves and seals any template alterations.

M: How else do the Sha support humanity?

C: They hold space on and under the Earth. He says when people say, "the spirit of Gaia," that's him. But also, they will stand in different places, and sometimes people will see them, or sense a large, heavy energy. And that's not a negative. It feels heavy because that's of their people. And they have a lower vibration, and that's not in a bad way.

He says he gets frustrated when he hears humans talk about "a high vibration" all the time. He wants us to know that the low vibration is assisting us as well to seal in templates and that. Not a low vibration equating to a negative energy, but you need all of the frequencies to create the song.

M: So, if I am hearing you correctly, you are saying that vibration and polarity are different. That someone can be of a positive polarity but still be of a lower vibration?

C: Not for humans. Not in the human being itself. With him and his entities, yes. Sometimes if you are feeling a heavy energy in a room, or outdoors especially (they are rarely indoors), just to acknowledge it and that that's okay. Some people will perceive it as negative. He says that sometimes my people will be standing outside, and humans will try to clear us. But they need to be there. It's funny because he says, we don't clear anyway (laughing).

M: What were the Sha's original mission on the planet? What was their beginning mission here?

C: We needed to lay a foundation and be the first vibrational frequency to arrive and be laid down and to be the holders of the original human template — the Christed mind. The original template. And be keepers of it. We hold it deeply within us so that it is protected and there is no other entity that can interfere with it. They can assist and it's up to our people to prove or disprove it and we also are to hold space on top of the planet as well so that other astral families can assist us when we observe vibrational shifts are needed. So, we are satellites, so to speak, in human terms.

M: The first time that I heard of the rock beings it was a ceremony

with a few other beings and they were taking, what the client described as, a citrine crystal, and then holding this ceremony and then the citrine and these rock beings were absorbed into this planet. And at the time they said this was the beginning of the Earth. And I have never really heard anything else about it. I am wondering if this feels connected and true. Or if there is something else you would like to correct?

C: *Very much so. That is our primary stone, but we are also keepers of all the others. There are other things that have come upon Earth. There is one green stone. We needed assistance because we were in a vibrational shift, and we were struggling and one of the astral families assembled us a new stone that came from outer space. That was the start of when the plan was laid out for the shift that we're experiencing now. But yes, that's very...we did...we were the creators of the Earth.*

R: **We wanted to know about the creation of the first humans on the Earth.**

M: **There are talks about human beings coming from Lyra being seeded onto the planet. I also know that there were times when humans were more in a Lightbody. Some call it the Adamic seed. I am wondering about the first time the humans were brought to the planet. What their bodies were like. What their consciousness was like?**

C: *When the families first collaborated, they were brought in their essence form. We needed to train some to do basic survival things. I am seeing four or five brought in at first. And then as they were able to thrive more were brought in. And they were brought into a denser jungle location where there would be plenty of vegetation for them to live off of. And fresh water. It almost seems like the Christian version of the Garden of Eden.*

M: **So first they came in in more of an essence form, like a Lightbody?**

C: *Yes.*

M: **And then how did it become more dense? What was that process? Moving into physicality.**

C: *The Families of Light worked together with the Sha to create the human body. We manifested it. We were able to manifest the thoughtform into matter. And we were a main aspect of that, and the human body needs to be heavier to stay here on Earth.*

Although it may have been able to be a bit lighter in the beginning, but we were the facilitator of that and that is why it's heavy.

Age of Expansion

As we can see, there is a system of higher evolutionary intelligence that is beyond the standard biological and geological evolution models accepted by mainstream science. Each domain within Creation is tended to by these benevolent forces, evolving each domain towards higher and higher harmony. Once the Earth and humanity have been liberated from the grips of the negatively polarized controllers, there will be an unprecedented revelation of technology, science, and philosophy to bring humanity into a new frontier of consciousness.

TWO

Star Family Legacy

Here is more of Matan's story from the perspective of his oversoul describing the Elohim, and the creation of the first male human form on a planet his group created named Aiden. When I tried to search for it on the internet to see if anyone else has written about it, I only came across the boy's name Aiden which is the name of a Celtic sun god which I thought was nice synchronicity. In the session, Matan meets another Elohim in a male human form named Leo who is his divine counterpart. Coincidently, in this life, Matan and Leo are gay males again!

Transcript: The First Male Form

HS: *The planet Aiden is a planet that Matan and Leo's Beings first created, where they started creating their first forms, and they came through as male. With that, they started creating other forms (material creations) with it. They came to form the first male forms when they were light beings. We must bring to your attention: everything is created in spirit first before it is manifested in a solid, physical form. Matan and Leo's souls had a job, and it was brought through the Creator, to bring on first male forms. Through their unveiling process, they were shown how their Being came into Creation and how they started creating together. This is a big part of their beings, of who they really are.*

This goes back to the first incarnation on the first planet that they were created on. This is the planet, what you call Aiden, and it consists of men. There are different themes throughout creation on different planets. There are some that have much diversity through them as your Earth planet. There are some that are just the same beings. Going into your other cosmic families, such as your Greys or Tall Ones, Tall White Ones — they all look alike. They're all the same. So, there was a planet that was created that was all of the human male forms. There are female planets of the same too, and then there are planets that came together to intermix them together.

Your current Earth that you live on is a manifestation of other star systems. Many planets came to this planet to bring the creations forth. This planet, as it is ascending, will be the pearl of this galaxy. It will be the garden planet of the galaxy that will home the diversity of life forms throughout all star systems in this galaxy.

M: What types of intentions were put into creating the first male forms?

HS: Pure love. Pure love. The male form originally is pure love and gentle. He is not what you see in your now upon the planet. Actually, quite the opposite.

M: How did males interact with each other?

HS: Very lovingly. They did not compete; they cooperated. They were fully conscious of one another, living in full consciousness. You must know, there are other planets that have just males on them. There is a vast spectrum of planets out there in this universe and other universes that have themes to them. Some just have male forms on them. This has been spoken of through other people of your world. You must remember the vastness of creation.

R: Was the male form brought to this Earth before the female, or...

HS: Yes, we are telling you this is the truth. We are part of that. And there were others that were part of that with us.

R: What was the first civilization that was created upon this planet?

HS: Well, we can take you back to the time of Lemuria. That is still, within your world, still folklore, but Lemuria is a very true civilization that did exist. But there were others that came even before that.

M: Before we go to these other earlier civilizations, I want to ask more questions about the original male form. How did the male form replicate in those early times, if there was not the opposite sex?

HS: They did not have to actually reproduce in the way you do in your world. It was more energetic, yes. There is physicality in other worlds where males can actually reproduce and bring on another male form.

M: So, what was the process like when it was simply energy?

HS: Two males coming together energetically with love, which they are already, and intent of creating another form. And then it was reproduced.

M: Was it reproduced in the body of one of the males?

HS: In some worlds, yes. In certain planets, yes. On others, no.

You must note that the male forms on other planets do not look like yours.

M: What's different?

HS: They are more pure. They are pure humans. They don't have the mixing you have in your world.

M: When you speak of mixing, do you mean galactic races?

HS: Yes. Meaning that they are not hybrids. They are a pure human male.

M: We were wondering what the purpose was for the homosexual man or the homosexual woman? Is there a story there?

HS: There are themes to planets. Many themes. Some themes aren't the same form. Where they all come collectively together and separate from the collective into the same form. Then they choose within that consciousness of that form what they want to create, how they want to live within the creation, their roles, their personalities. It's a very beautiful thing.

M: Gay people have had a really hard time on this planet.

HS: Matan carries answers to that. We were all once the same, which we all really are. That is the cosmic joke of it. We take on so many forms, but there are first forms in Creation. There is an order in Creation when things are manifesting. Matan helped with the creation of the gay male. He was also shown about the gay human woman. Or what you would call gay in your world. It is just the same forms interacting on a certain level for an experience. This is what they have chosen, but it is a big part of Creation. This planet has been backward for some time now. For when it was first formed, there were the first forms of the same, that looked the same, that grouped together. Then came other forms that were different that came together. Then it branched out from that.

M: So, you are sharing with me…maybe I am getting this incorrectly, at first there was the same gender, the same sex together and then it was opposite?

HS: Yes.

M: Then we started creating from that? Creating other life forms? Creating other humans?

HS: Yes. That is where humanity has gotten things wrong.

M: Tell me about the first humans.

HS: They were gentle. Very gentle. They did not know violence. Then, an energy came in and created something where they fell from grace, and there are ones of us that decided to depart. There are ones that decided to stay. Oh, things got all scrambled up. Too much. Too many differences. So, he left the planet with other beings. He did not die.

R: In the Jewish Bible, there is a story of Adam, the man that took his

rib and created the female. Can you share your perspective about the creation of the female and human life on Earth?

HS: There are other beings that came in to help create the female. Once the female was created, then there was a force that came through, that chose to manifest them on the Earth plane. It's not as everyone thinks, through the rib of Adam; that is a metaphor to be used. We must remind you, there have been many civilizations on this planet that go back further. Everyone has questions pertaining to the story of Adam and Eve. There is some truth to this. Yes. As there are many gardens on this planet that were created when it was first created.

R: Can you set the record straight?

HS: We want to give you clarity on this without confusion. As you know of Lemuria, that time was a special time on this planet. When Lemuria was created, in the time of Atlantis, those were civilizations on this planet, but there were others too. There were many gardens and things set into Creation. So, when you have your souls that speak of the Adam and Eve story, there is truth for them on their soul path for that. In the manifestation of Creation, it's part of the Creator putting that set forth in Creation.

M: Yes. So, there were more creations before Adam and Eve?

HS: Yes. A lot more...many, MANY!

Ancestral Genetic Lines of the Milky Way

In one of my sessions, I learned of a group called the Carans or Carians, said to be the oldest species in the Orion constellation, who were described as an ancient negative polarity, service-to-self species who travel the universe in search of planets to plunder and species to control. When I did an internet search about them after the session, I read a few different descriptions of this group that had similarities to the sharing my client gave but also some differences. I had a slight hesitancy in sharing this data as I like to get information from several sources to verify the information. I have decided to include this information because I received it from a client that I trust deeply. I wonder if they even call themselves by this name. I decided that the archetype of progenitor and the intentions put into their genetic creations and experimentations was the important part of the story.

Receiving this information was a profound experience for me that opened up my mind to a more expansive understanding of the ancient Milky

Way history. I'm sure there is much more to learn and understand and more clarity will come as we move down the Ascension timeline.

These service-to-self beings would be described as reptilian in appearance and created what is commonly called the Draconian species which are from the constellation of Draco; the Draconians eventually created what is commonly called the Reptilian race. The Reptilian genetic coding was later permitted by Source to be inserted into the human genome as a way of expanding their genetic line in this region of space. The Reptilian DNA is what gives humanity the ego so that it can have individual consciousness, competitiveness, and the drive to protect itself.

The Carans, which are never up to any good, created the Draconian race by merging the highly intelligent and spiritual expression of the dragon DNA — yes, they are real — with the primitive intelligence of the dinosaur DNA. Dragons are defenders of the realms and "rule over" entire regions of space by tending to the energetics and protecting their territory from invaders. The Carans basically wanted to create a dumbed-down dragon that was self-serving and very powerful. This Draconian species would be an army that would rule over the region of Orion for the Carans. From the perspective of these cold-hearted rulers, the more species they can control, the more power they have which is a complete inversion of power of true creator beings that are working in unison with the Divine. The client's Higher Self said that at a certain point the Draconians ruled over 800 species in the Orion constellation.

The Draconians were described as having reptile-like features, wrinkly faces, and protruding spikes on their face with stocky bodies. They have a high frequency and high consciousness capacity like the dragons but with a primal, instinctual consciousness like the dinosaurs. Even though these beings operate at a higher consciousness, I was told Eighth Dimensional, they lack an emotional body, which makes them purely analytical and focused on the next steps in their agenda with no emotional hang-ups. Although, it was said that the Draconians do have a touch of feminine energy to them and that they do have a capacity to grow in love. The beings that created this species were curious about what would happen if a being were given a high consciousness but had no reference of cause and effect, no empathy. This is unlike humans who are mentally preoccupied with how people relate to them on an emotional level. These Draconians are more goal-oriented without the duality that comes with emotions. This type of service-to-self consciousness is quite different than humans on the Earth who do things, as backward as it may seem at times, to acquire more love and emotional safety. This does not mean that the Draconians are not connected to the Divine; their connection is just felt differently than a heart-centered species who consciously choose to work towards a greater harmony for All. Both polarities exist to create dynamics for interaction and evolution of consciousness.

Eventually, the Draconians created a more commonly known race called the Reptilians as a lower-dimensional expression and hybridization of the Draconians. While many humans on the Earth in modern times hold a negative perspective of the Reptilian race, I have had several clients who regressed to lifetimes of living as a Reptilian or a Draconian as their soul wanted to experience being on the "dark side," or the other side of the conflict, for the purpose of spiritual growth and knowledge. I was quite surprised to learn that the Reptilian races have the capacity to grow in love and compassion and ascend in their own consciousness. Clients described Reptilians who carry love in their hearts, have loving families, and have their own evolutionary process to awaken to higher love. We are quick to pass judgment on beings from our limited perspective from not having the bigger story. I find that once we hear the other side of the story, we often grow in understanding and compassion. Even in human history, we see examples of people and groups of people committing terrible acts believing that, in doing so, they were protecting their family or nation.

Lyrans, from the constellation of Lyra, are Earth humanity's ancient ancestors and the first humanoid species in our region of space. The Lyrans also seeded Earth with the first humans using 144,000 oversouls from the Lyran lineage. I have heard of pure Lightbody forms and angelic beings, as well as hybrid humanoids that have arms, legs, and a torso like humans but are mixed with feline genetics. We can see some of these beings in the Ancient Egyptian statues from when these beings visited the Earth in the past.

Long ago, much longer than humans can comprehend, an intergalactic war began between beings from the constellation of Orion and beings from Lyra. Factions of beings in service-to-self consciousness from Orion attempted to take over the Lyran civilization for their own gain. This intergalactic battle was a war over resources and consciousness. The Reptilians not only wanted to take over the Lyran system but wanted to infiltrate and control the Lyran consciousness through mind control tactics and energy devices. It was one of those wars that went on for so long that many forgot why they were even fighting and there were many casualties on all sides.

This story causes a lot of judgment against Reptilian beings, especially because some Draconian/Reptilian ancestral lines have been using these same tactics against the people of Earth. It was shared in one of Ron's sessions that it is two ancient Reptilian family lines that have been controlling humanity for thousands of years. This is the tyrannical force and distorted consciousness behind the mainstream institutions like the Vatican, the banking systems, sick-for-profit industries, and other institutions that keep humanity in poverty, race wars, and mind control. That being said, the power has always been in humanity's hands to stand in sovereignty or give in to outside authority and tyranny. Jesus is called the "Redeemer" because he came to show humanity the pathway out from the slave mindset so that we could break free of these shadow controllers.

The Reptilian race has mostly evolved beyond service-to-self into a service-to-all consciousness and is supporting humanity now in our grand transition. Some will have a hard time releasing the charged narrative about Reptilians because they hold polarity and victim consciousness within their being and do not have all sides of the story. All characters have played a role in the unfolding of our galactic story to assist the expansion of galactic collective consciousness. That being said, it is suggested to use discernment through the power of the heart when engaging in communication with any beings to ensure that they hold the highest intentions for the engagement. This applies to physical interactions as well as astral and psychic interactions.

The Lyran home planet was described as a beautiful paradise teeming with life. Technology was used by the Orion group that destroyed this paradisaical Lyran planet. The loss of this planet is still felt within the heart of the souls of those who had lifetimes on the destroyed planet. Many humans that were souls incarnated as Lyrans when the planet was destroyed still experience high sensitivity to radiation and electromagnetic frequency pollution. Their etheric DNA, the higher dimensional form of DNA, still holds significant radiation from this cataclysm.

Transcript: Destruction of Lyran Civilization

The following session is from Krissa, a somnambulistic client. Krissa's consciousness began to fade away as I asked for more information. As this happened, the feline Lyran aspect of her Oversoul began to incorporate fully through her vessel. When this happened, Krissa said her consciousness was "floating" around in the background and could sometimes hear what her body was communicating but it was not coming from "her." It became emotional as her Lyran aspect began to cry over the loss of her beloved home planet.

C: *I'm walking on a white, stone path. There's a quality of the light that is far more brilliant and I'm wearing a long, white garment with sandals on. It's not the same kind of solid matter that is experienced on Earth in the third dimension. I see now there are beautiful, white stone buildings that are luminous and iridescent in color. Almost an ivory-colored stone building, and I keep hearing the words: Orion, Orion.*

M: Let's get a little bit more familiar with your body. You said you were wearing this white material and sandals. Become more familiar with your body and describe it to me.

C: *This is amazing. I'm a beautiful being of feline fur and body, very tall, coverings of the feet. Sandals for the feline feet and the walking on two feet like a human. There's a piece of me that is so scared to see this because it feels like home. I feel like my heart's going to break. It hurts so bad. I can do it; I can do it.*

I am about to deliver the sad news to the elders, the other Lyran elders. I'm an oracle. I'm so old and my physical body isn't as strong as it used to be. I'm thousands of years old in this body. I have foreseen and others have foreseen various timeline possibilities, that beings from the Orion system are not to be trusted; they will ruin our world. We will be at war, but it has not yet come to pass, that a critical tipping point has come into the consciousness of myself and other seers where we must report the findings, and it grieves us very greatly. It grieves us to do so because we did not want...we spent our lives trying to shift the consciousness away from this outcome, away from this tipping point. Yet we have failed and all that we see before us will crumble and we must leave now.

I feel the shadows of many, many lifetimes in this world. Forward and backward, I feel my consciousness stretched between twelve dimensions. And when it is thus, an even higher angelic emanation harkening back to closer to the origin of Source consciousness itself. I see that all is well. I see that all is well, yet the part of me that deeply loves this world and all that it stands for feels that it will break and shatter and that a thousand lifetimes of tears won't be enough to grieve it adequately. There's so much to hold, so much to say, so much to do and express. I am tired. I am ready to do this final piece of my work and let this body pass, pass beyond the threshold again.

M: You were saying that there were beings from Orion that aren't to be trusted? Is that true?

C: They're walking through a cycle that is a world not so different from the Earth at the present time you see, with lessons of contrast and duality. Lessons of separation and greed and wanting to define that there is a...all beings exist on an arc of ascent and descent. Predictable cycles of emanation from Source. Lower than Elohim and angelic emanations and then Ascended Masters and things like this and into the body; this is from an Earth point of reference. So, this cycle of emanation on the arc of descent is going from the Oneness, that Source Consciousness, to various emanations moving down the dimensional levels. The arc of ascent is what the Earth is on now. At the moment of time Orion had been on an arc of descent and it still existed in dimensions six through three, you see what I say, they had descended, and they were on an arc of descent having to iterate fully the division, the "us and them," the hatred, the wanting, the greed, the destruction. They had to do this, you see, that was part of what that world was meant to learn and teach. So much could be said about this, yet I have seen that I will have lifetimes helping them back up the arc of ascent. I don't want to. I would choose not, yet the larger piece of me knows that it is part of my soul's path, and I will accept it gladly.

M: I'm wondering what we would call that group here on the Earth? Do we have a name for this group?

C: All of the names that have been said on Earth don't really fully express that this was a FACTION of beings. A large faction. But a faction of beings that gained traction. Some were humanoid. Some Reptilian. Many Reptilians were not of this ilk. There are many Reptilians that are positive or neutral. We would say these words are an oversimplification, but we say these words for our purposes, you see. But there were a number of, you see, humanoid beings, reptile beings that were part of that lower denominator of consciousness that had to iterate out polarity to its extreme. Do you see?

M: I understand, yeah.

C: *And people use the word here Archons. They use the word like a vampiric, a very draining like enslavement. Words like...um... creating a trick around to harvest and utilize lower vibrational energy for their own purposes. This was part of the situation. They want to do that to Lyra. They want to do that, but we will leave. They can have the buildings, the container; they can have the planet as much as it grieves me, but they will not harvest; they will not enslave; they will not hijack our consciousness. We will leave and we will build anew. And then my soul will incarnate in another star system for the purposes of helping to elevate. This is a cycle of ascent and descent, yet it is part of a bigger plan. A bigger, divine order.*

In the journey of rediscovering the nature of self as creator gods and goddesses, we must first see our power to create entropy, destruction, despair, and annihilation collectively. And then relearn the power to create life, to create connection, to create elevation, ascension. So, this was a downward arc in the Orion system; they are not for the most part...they are back. They have ascended from that.

Everybody that I love and care for deeply is inside a spaceship ready to go. I don't want to go to Vega as I want to die here, and now my body is so close to expiring you see. But they, they do not trust; they're not ready to let me go. My children, my grandchildren. The priests and priestesses and seers that I taught and mentored. And I'm so tired and they're putting me in this spaceship, and I rest and wait for the process of propulsion to go; body drops into a stasis while this happens, folding space and time like an accordion. Folding into a pocket of altered gravity, you understand. Travel. So tired... The individuals listened; they mostly almost all listened to us, and we know it is the correct information to leave and go re-establish the Pleiades. We know this will come to pass; it will be well. I'm dying.

Transcript: The Oracle of Orion

Here is a client named Tina that regressed to a lifetime as an oracle in the Orion civilization. As the oracle, she would sit in a room far from the influences of other beings and channel information that would help the Orion group during the great war. In previous sessions, she shared about the black cube and black pyramid technology that is installed on planets for harvesting negative energy for nefarious technology and deeds. They describe the black cube in Mecca and the black pyramid in Las Vegas as being part of this negative extraterrestrial energy harvesting network. The client also mentioned a solar flash event that is similar to what we will experience here on the Earth as we ascend. I took some time to ask about the cause of the Orion Wars.

C: *So, the technology of the black pyramids came from somewhere up in that Orion's belt. They would fight the same way that, say you have two people who, like maybe the Jews and Palestine, like fighting to the death. It's a tribe like that. So, you have these tribes. And they would fight to the point where they would obliterate each other, their whole DNA line, just total annihilation. And what would they learn from that genocide? They did this for millennia, back and forth, back and forth, back and forth. So, what changed them was that their sun 'burped,' and it blew open a bunch of third eyes at once. It 'burped' them open... It's more like gas; it's more like a belch and it burped, and it blew the tops off some people. Their physical body popped off; their top popped off. They don't look quite like us. But their top popped off. And this changed them.*

The war was over technology. It was so long. I mean, you think of the Hundred Year War, the War of the Roses, a multi-generational war, a war that went on so long that nobody can remember why it started. You just remember, you just don't like that other side. Nobody can remember why. So, that's because nobody can remember why. We're going to get over it now.

M: **So, the humans now are ending that collective war by finding peace with themselves?**

C: *Yes. And so that war that was started in Orion is coming to an end now. Like it was always on the end date. It's been ending, but the actual period at the end of the sentence will be like, the end. Period.*

M: **And how is the war from Orion...how does that influence the war that's happening here on Earth?**

C: *So, the tribes from Orion, the tribes from Earth are the descendants of the tribes from Orion. So, in some ways, some of those people, they would just destroy things, just totally obliterate them. So, in order to escape their technology, they had to come. Some of those tribes came to Earth to start the tribes here. This might sound controversial. I don't want to make anyone upset. So, even if it isn't actually able to be proven that the DNA is from them, they carried the codes in a way. Or the incarnation codes to incarnate. So, you were talking about Abraham and his sons and the tribes of Abraham. He was holding that [coding], you know, and then King David and all of that. And you look at those old kings and they held a higher frequency than the average person on this planet. And that was true. You might today, if you met them, it wouldn't maybe feel that different because more people are higher on the ascension. But back then there weren't that many people that had higher thought.*

So, what happened? There was almost complete genocide in Orion. The oversouls of the Twelve Tribes wanted another chance to try to work it out. And so, it's almost like we were talking the other day about "the most impossible thing." Is it peace in the Middle East? It's not that impossible when you think about it, because they all come from the same tribe, in a sense, back, back, back, back, back. But the original argument had to do with those black pyramids and the original argument was over power and technology. One group thought they were better than the other group and then tried to get domination and power over them. And then that didn't work. And then they had the 'burp' and then that changed them. And then after that, things were different, but they wanted to test it. It is a test. It's a test of energy to see if they can come together. The test of energy is if those oversouls can split apart into twelve tribes and see if they can come together.

So, they did all this before on another planet, almost destroyed it, right? Some of them escaped. Some of them didn't. Some of them started over. Then they did it again somewhere. So, you have the Orion wars. So, you have a lot of battling, different battling factors. So, you have invading tribes coming and basically ripping down the culture of another existing planet. It was gnarly.

M: What about the Orion civilizations and how they interacted with the Lyrans, with the cats?

C: Well, that's what she's seeing is the cats are ripping her out of the temple. I see lions that are taking her out of the temple, like RIPPING her out of the temple. But she's the oracle so she doesn't see well. That doesn't make sense. She doesn't physically see well. I mean, she may be blind as the oracle. So, she can't see them, but she can smell them. And so that lion smell. Why did they do that? I think they ripped the oracle out because the oracle, they thought, was what was giving away their secrets or giving away their next move. They could see their next move. She could see the next move. It was strategic. It was a military strategic thing. They were angry. I want to call them lions, but the Lyrans were angry. So, their technology started to outpace their human...not their humanity...but what makes you compassionate or what makes your empathy. So that it's almost like you would say, like in a sci-fi movie where an AI would take over something like that. It was sort of like that. So that the frequency that was given off, like when we were talking about the brainwaves and how certain frequencies are given off and that's what creates the ascension. The theta waves. The waves were being manipulated. That was one of the weapons going back and forth. They were blasting each other with different brainwave weapons.

So, the Lyrans showed up and they cleared everybody out. Just killed everybody. This is a long time ago. The Lyrans are not like that now. I mean, everybody's passed this, people are past this now. This is billions of years ago. A lot of time. I'm seeing 2.4 something. Million? Billion? It's a long time ago. It's a long time ago.

M: Well, when people speak about Earth being under the control of Dark Forces, is that connected to this Orion war?

C: So, because those planets went through their ascension, the frequency of the biology couldn't hold lower frequencies like war and hate and things. But Earth was still compatible with that. I mean, it's not as much now as it was. So that's the difference. You know we've shifted; we shifted things here. And so now the frequency won't hold things. That's why all this stuff is coming to the surface. For millennia, we've had child abuse, but now we're angry about it and taking to the streets about it. That is the same. It's just now the frequency...when we go through our ascension here, then things won't be able to manifest here. They'll go somewhere else; they'll go to the next...and it's not...I mean, I know it feels very, like right and wrong, because I'm not saying that it's right to have murder and abuse. But I'm just saying it's part of the duality. It's part of this ascension process as far as it creates a catalyst for another planet to go through what you've gone through. But there won't be a great war again. I know people think things are getting worse, but there won't...

The war that you're in now, and you're in war right now, is very covert, like COVID covert. COVID is not a disease. It's the name of the war. So, your war is just not obvious to you. And that's part of what the dark side likes about it. Because then they tell you, you're not at war. What are you talking about? You're not at war. You're crazy. But you're not crazy. You're at war. It's a war. And so, there's so much happening behind the scenes, you know, on all levels. And so, it's good because victory is coming; victory is coming soon.

More Intergalactic Races

Another group that I heard about was the Aldebarans from the constellation of Taurus which is close to Orion. One of these beings was described as a black-blue-skinned humanoid, with brown hair, and electric blue eyes. This species is a highly intelligent, family-oriented, loving species. These peacekeepers worked with the Pleiadians and the Lyrans to push back the Reptilian group during the Orion wars and stop the destruction.

Many of the ascension wayshowers had incarnations on both sides of the conflict. Some played the villain, and some played the victims. This karma balanced on Earth now is the finalization of the greater galactic karma reaching back billions of years throughout our Milky Way galaxy. The way it was simplified to me was that God was like "You cannot keep destroying everything. All of you go to Earth, incarnate as humans, and settle your issues." So, it seems like that is the task for humanity, to release our perceived differences and our various self-serving agendas and come together as one family in one heart.

Beings who could escape Lyra before the cataclysm spread throughout the galaxy as refugees looking for a new home. These beings seeded new Lyran outposts in the areas of the stars Sirius A and Sirius B, in the Canis Major constellation, the Andromeda galaxy, the Pleiades star cluster, and maybe other regions. These beings were received and cared for by different intelligent species living in those systems. These star races shared healing technologies and began to create hybrid species using the Lyran DNA.

Besides the Lyrans, Pleiadians, and Sirians, our allies include the Arcturians from the star region of Arcturus in the Bootes constellation. I have also heard of the Blue Avians, which are blue, bird-like humanoid beings. I have mostly had clients regress to Blue Avian lives at the beginning of the seeding of Earth and the beginning stages of New Earth development. Maybe part of their purpose is using their ability to fly to watch over new experiments and report back to the higher councils how the progress is moving along.

I have also heard of "the Greys" who were permitted to experiment on human DNA to create hybrids for the seeding of other worlds. Although, I heard that they are not permitted to do these experiments anymore because it got too out of control. Most of the time, "abduction" is an experience that has been agreed upon by the soul before incarnation. Many starseeds are taken aboard spacecraft to have DNA repairs or updates to their consciousness to support the ascension. Even if the mainstream news and governments push the story of a threat of alien invasion, we must remember the negative ETs are already here and control the mainstream narrative. The positive ETs are here as well, and they would never allow a negative ET invasion at this stage of the ascension.

I have had clients describe civilizations in many other regions of space, including even more distant star systems and other universes. This universe is teeming with intelligent life with many advanced species who have existed for trillions of years and likely more. Humanity (on planet Earth) is still quite young when we compare our species with the other star races and planetary systems' legacies. When we shift to New Earth, our star brethren will return and teach us many new things to advance life on planet Earth. We have so much to look forward to!

THREE

The Earth Experiment

Over a long time, Earth's physicality was formed and eventually infused with its own soul essence. Earth, our beloved Gaia, is a living, breathing sentient being of Light. Beyond her physicality, she has a soul with an evolutionary destiny pathway and plan, just like you and me, that is per the Divine Plan of Source. The soul of Gaia had other lifetimes leading up to a graduation phase where she was initiated into a higher level of soul ascension that meant that she was ready to hold life. Many cosmic beings gathered on the planet's cooling surface after the volcanic phase to perform a grand ceremony where Gaia infused herself into the planet as life-giving water was poured across the surface to bring life.

Transcript: Activation of Gaia

This next client takes us to the beginning of the seeding process to a grand ceremony to activate the Life of Gaia!

C: *I'm wearing all white and there's a golden room around. It feels like a sacred space. And there's water. There are people in robes bathing and steam and flowers. It smells really beautiful. Incense.*

M: **Are you alone there or are there others with you?**

C: *It's full of people and people are laughing. Music playing. I see that someone is playing a harp. It's a celebration. It goes outside. Again, a long environment. It goes as far as a football field. I'm at the top of this waterfall again. It looks like Pangea before everything changed. I'm back to the beginning of the planet. We're all here at the beginning for the birthing of the planet, and the birth of the planet comes when the waterfall came into this planet. We earned it. The planet has the badges. She earned this. Gaia was a young woman once. She earned this ability, and the Gods blessed her.*

M: **You were saying that Gaia needed to do some things to earn her badges. Tell me what that means.**

C: *I'm saying that she had earned them and that's why she became a planet. And that's why she got to be our mother. What an honor it is for her. To have come so far in the universe to have gained the trust of the stars and all of its people. All of the sacredness and all of the things that are here in Gaia. We're like a treasure box. We are this special thing, and we have no idea how sacred we are. How special we are. Gaia trained for a long time to be strong enough to hold us on her back. Running through obstacles and shooting arrows. Warrior. Many lifetimes Gaia lived before she was able to be strong enough to hold this. I see Gaia is a true daughter of the Creator.*

Transcript: Beginning of Earth

This dear soul is the one who brought me into the world of Quantum Healing by following his intuition and sharing *The Three Waves of Volunteers and the New Earth* by Dolores Cannon with me. This session still teaches me something new every time I read it. It truly is a living transmission! This client describes himself as a being that I now understand to be one of the Sha although he never said that term in our session.

C: *I guess it's like magma all around me. Like a planet full of fire and different craters...not craters, but like how on Earth when it dries out it cracks; it's like that except in between all the cracks is red magma.*

M: Is there any plant life there?

C: *There's no plant life. There doesn't seem to be life. I seem to be a kind of rock figure. Like a...I'm like a little humanoid rock. I'm like gray and brown stone. Four toes and like a stone for the lower part of the leg. A little joint. Bigger stones for thighs. I don't see any genitalia, but there's a butt. Kind of a round belly.*

M: Do you have anything in your hands?

C: *On one hand, I have...my right hand I have a violet crystal. In my left hand, I have two blue stones that look like sapphires.*

M: What do these stones do?

C: *They're glowing. Across in the distance, there's a yellow, looks like a spire, a pyramid, shining really brightly. It actually looks like...it's like a soft, white glow is coming off of it, and it's hardening the ground. It's bringing life. And plants. And water.*

M: What do you do with most of your day?

C: *I think I have been surveying the growth of the planet.*

M: So, you are a steward there? Caretaker?

C: I think so.

M: How did you get there? Were you born there?

C: I think I am. Yeah. I'm manifested from the planet. It's giving birth to life.

M: So, what would you like to do next?

C: Well, I think I need to go over to the spire with the crystals. Standing in front of it. It's very tall. It's a giant citrine crystal. Sticking out of the earth, actually goes all the way through it. I'm there with other beings like me. We all have crystals of different, varying colors, and we're putting them onto the citrine crystal.

M: What does that do?

C: It activates it. I think we've been waiting a very long time to do this. And we've all gathered there; we're putting the crystals into the citrine. Citrine's dissolving.

M: Is this a good thing?

C: Yes. The planet's calming. It's a feeling of love (begins crying). It's a very positive feeling. The crystal is being absorbed by the planet, and we're going in with it. We're dying. And this is what we came here to do. I'm being drawn to the center of the planet. We become the planet itself. And it's starting to grow life. Volcanoes are erupting. The shimmering, yellow glow is going again; it's disappearing. Planet's starting to spin. I can see it going around its sun. All the giant crystals are coming out of the planet.

M: And what do these crystals do?

C: They're sending beams of light out into the universe, in all directions, in all colors.

M: Where do these beams go?

C: To different solar systems. It seems that everything's getting drawn in. Getting closer and closer and they explode to come together and explode. Everything's shattering into a million crystals. Looks like a nuclear explosion, except it's a rainbow crystal. Flowing outward in a disc.

M: What happens to these crystals next?

C: They're getting sucked back into a core. It's Earth.

Creating Planets

Once a planet moves beyond the volcanic phase and begins to cool, a web of mycelial species, fungus, is put on the surface to lay the foundational grid of life force energy. The mushrooms act as a neural pathway to pulse vital energy across the planet's surface so that other, more advanced biological forms can be introduced and connected through the network. This network bridges with the greater pathways of Light connecting all of the planets, stars, galaxies, and beyond to the Source. From there other life forms can be introduced.

Over long periods of time, millions upon millions of years, Earth was tended to, nurtured, and matured by the support of ultraterrestrial and extraterrestrial beings working together with a unified vision directed by Source Intelligence. A theme was chosen for the planet of "seeking harmony within diversity," and many varieties of species and DNA were brought to Earth from many different areas of the universe to interact, grow, and evolve in the paradisiacal and diverse environment of Earth. These cosmic scientists watch and observe the planet allowing the magic of evolution to unfold within the grand Earth experiment, occasionally visiting the surface to check on their precious creation.

Transcript: Young Earth

Here is another transcription from a session with Matan speaking about the seeding of life on Earth.

M: How was early civilization created between the animals and the plants and the beings of the planet?

HS: When the planet was brought into creation, many plants and animals were brought from other planets, through other star systems. Not everything originated here. Other planets have been in Creation much longer than this Earth. This Earth of yours is new still, but at the same time old as time progresses. Not as old as other planets in your star system. Many other beings from other planets have brought many things to contribute to this planet. Is this making sense for you?

R: Yes.

M: How many other planets were sourced from for these creations here?

HS: Several. Several. If you knew how many beings were actually in this part of your universe, you would be amazed. And they are around this planet, not everyone can see them. At times people can, and at times people can't.

M: Tell me about how human beings came to be on this planet. Early human forms.

HS: *You must know that humans of this planet came from other planets. The human form came from other planets, other star systems. There are humans in other star systems. You are not the only humans.*

Transcript: Overseeing the Beginning of Earth

This next client was taken to a lifetime at the beginning of the Earth Experiment. The client described her body as having lizard feet with three toes that were webbed together. She was not wearing clothing but remarked about iridescent, green-blue scaled skin, and long, thin legs. She described herself as slightly androgynous but leaning more towards masculine expression. She felt younger but a bit flat in vital energy as though her body was not meant for the Earth's environment. The top of her head came to a crest like a mohawk that went over the top of the head and faded as it descended the spine. Her face had a pointed beak with eyes that were oval-shaped under a heavy brow. She held in her hands a defense weapon that resembled a harpoon or arrow. She wore a necklace with a medallion that denoted her rank.

As she looked around herself, she described a desolate lava field with little vegetation. The land was dark; the sky was dark; and the scene felt "moody." On her left side, she saw and felt the ocean and all around her wrapped the black lava field. She had a sense that she was guarding, protecting, or keeping watch.

She lived alone in her "watchtower," a structure made of crystalline material and simple rock that was formed into several intersecting diamond shapes framed with wood. There was a hole in the ground where she could acquire fish from the ocean which she ate raw.

M: I want you to see what you do with most of your time in that life. What do you see, what do you do?

C: *Ok, now I am seeing... Well, the first thing that came to mind is a fire — a light. I am a fire or a light. I am the guardian of that fire.*

M: What's the significance of this fire?

C: *It feeds down, through the land, into the center of the planet. It's a representative...I can't think of the right word. Flame vibration. Emissary? Of the planet. I protect it. I keep watch over it and protect it to make sure it keeps emitting its vibration.*

M: What is this vibration used for?

C: It constructs things. It slowly...it gives, it informs step-by-step the biological processes that existing organisms respond to. Allowing them to...not just mutate and grow but embody and contain the foundational information they need to exist on the surface and support what will then come next.

M: So, it's a very important energy there.

C: Yes. It comes from the heart spring.

M: The heart spring of what?

C: The Earth.

NEXT SCENE: BROADCASTING FLOWERS

M: Where are you?

C: It's like a texture is all I'm seeing. Like a sloping blue shape of...not blue, blueish...it's like elephant skin or something like that type of texture, but it's so strange. Everything is soft. I am in dark. If I reach out to touch or lean into the structure like it's a hill, it's squishy. It has a softness to it.

M: Let's zoom out so we can get a bigger perspective on it. What do you see as you zoom out?

C: A flower. A purply, bluish flower. And so, from where I just came from, my awareness was inside of it — pushing against the petals.

M: Why were you inside of this flower?

C: This is the same veins into the heart space of the planet; it's the same access. The flower center has the same light.

M: What does it do for you to connect with the flower this way?

C: I'm just happy that they're multiplying, broadcasting, and becoming. They are torchbearers, in a sense, of this vibrational frequency, replicating and sending out higher and wider. I feel proud and happy for it. This is why growing things are attracted to growing things. All tapped into the essence of vibrational encodement.

M: What kind of codes are coming from this flower?

C: That's what is interesting. They're so many transmissions that we're not even necessarily aware of.

M: What's the function of these transmissions? You can share a few of them.

C: This particular flower informs. It has to do with way of being, growth, and openness. It has something to do with openness. This balance of...it's like the Tao, the balance of fire and water. The growth, the reaching, the striving, and the receptivity. Ebb and flow. Allowing. They kind of hold...it's holding that Light of the Tao, of perfect balance. And they're all, if I zoom further up, there is so much communication. It's so striking. There's a world of transaction — the giving and the receiving. It's a group effort. Each one holds a thread of this heart flame, and together it's a group effort to make it larger and more spread out. By making it thinner and wider. As they communicate with each other, they're informing each other as well. They're not singular. They have become, in a sense, their own self-protectors, but they don't need to protect anymore because of that network. It's self-evident, I want to say. It is. It cannot be bothered.

M: What was the purpose of that life?

C: Foundation and formulation. Helping just maintain and steady the foundations of creation of this place. And tending to the formulation, not creating, but it's almost like gardening. Where things need to be just pruned or tended a little bit, keeping things on track. This was almost like a lab lifetime. It was like honing, testing and honing, fine-tuning.

MEETING HER COUNCIL OF GUIDES

C: There are four entities, nonphysical. Patches of light, they're light basically. There's just all darkness, not a room. Half of the entities on the left, there are four in front of me. The two on the left are quiet. The two on the right are more involved in this. The two on the left feel more...they all feel cosmic, but the two on the left feel less concerned with matter. The two on the right are the bridge between spirit and matter, more creation-oriented in a physical sense. I just see them more invested in whatever this is; they're more involved.

M: What's being discussed there? What's happening in this group?

C: The idea or the agreement is being made around incarnating in some kind of physical form in order to... The dialogue is around the physical form in order to be involved directly in the physical creation. Through obviously an energetic source and impulse, that's where everything comes. There is something about it that, for me, feels unusual or foreign to do that, but there is something necessary about being in the body with this distribution of this heart vein — light source.

M: What's unique? Why must you be in physical form? What was needed?

C: It's also to see how it affects the physical bodies. I think I am culturing DNA in my own body as well. I am experiencing them watching this for other life forms. In the proximity to guarding that flame, or sitting with and being around that flame, I was also...am also...going to be receiving the pure encodement of the planetary body so that life can be on it. There are the DNA and the cellular structures. There has to be some cultivation of dense body tissue in order to be a dense planet. There have to be access points in those structures for non-density as well, for this pure energy to move and cleanse and clear this cultivated physical tissue and DNA and cellular, nervous systems.

M: So, once you cultivate this DNA, once you gather all this information to make the changes, what will this DNA be used for in the future? How is it used?

C: This is somehow interwoven into what becomes different life forms on Earth. In particular, the different races of beings who are meant to hold space for the physical life forms and be the custodians of the physical life forms, and continually be integrating spirit into the cellular networks of themselves and the structures around them. Like the flowers we were looking at, everything is resonating and vibrating with everything else. There is never a moment when there isn't information moving between cellular structures. Anything, everything that is the planet and life on the planet is emitting cross-coding frequencies. They are needed to be...like labs where this movement of energy through different types of tissue and structures was not quite tested but tried in different ways. The way the structures work isn't quite... The network initially was supposed to be more open — even with the concept of density. It's slightly muddied, or more blocked.

M: What caused it to be muddied or blocked?

C: There is some kind of contamination. Like too much involvement somehow. I'm not super clear. There was more involvement very early on that gave a thicker...I keep saying "cellular structure," so I guess it's cells. Everything should be slightly more porous ideally, but it went forward with the thicker structure. Just in hope it could be alleviated at some point along the way. There are continued moments in time where there is an alleviation and then thickening. It goes back and forth a little bit.

M: I want you to see what was causing that initial disturbance. You said there was involvement earlier on. Do you have access to what that was? What do you see there?

C: Totally, my area of focus I can feel, but there's some kind of a wave. Not a liquid wave but a wave pushing in from outside very early on. That wasn't part of the plan. It's almost like catching a cold. That kind of infection, something came from outside. Outside what was the initial idea. I see it.

M: What does it look like?

C: It looks like a darkish cloud, but it just feels like it doesn't fit. It feels like when two people don't get each other — it's the kind of discord. That this powder, this thickness, this vibration...it's essentially a vibration but pretty powerful infiltration of a vibration that doesn't have anything to do with the existing what was created. What was created is stronger and bigger than this...it feels like a virus to me.

M: How did it affect the planet? What did it do once it arrived?

C: In this analogy, it's like when the body is fighting something that doesn't belong there. The planet begins to do that too because it doesn't belong there. And so, in this early moment — early, early, infantile stage of things, the template of conflict is seeded because it's trying to evict this disharmonious vibration. Disharmony becomes a part of the story, and then the next part of the story is how to harmonize out of disharmony, at every level.

M: So, it sounds like this energy affected all layers of evolution on this planet.

C: Yes.

M: What was being done to balance this, from your perspective?

C: You can see how from within the Earth's core-essence, there is still this overwhelmingly huge web of life that functions perfectly, even in its chaotic states. It's in the perfect state of balance. And so, it, oh...there's continued amplification from the core through these kinds of veins of energy through to the surface. It's from the inside out that it's healing itself. It's so similar in what is called the "New Age," the conversation is always that if you want to heal something, you go inside and heal from the inside out, the same principle. The same. The self-realization of one's own core of light amplifying from the center through to the surface and radiating outward to cleanse and clear the whole space around.

HIGHER SELF CONVERSATION

M: Wonderful. So, out of all the lifetimes you could have shown her today, why did you show this particular life?

HS: To give her a sense of her place in the order of things. How she fits into structures of creation. How she is involved when sometimes she doesn't think she's involved — a sense of being in life.

M: The next scene you showed was with her exploring this big flower and the network of energies that come from the Earth's core up through these flowers into the atmosphere. Why did you show this to her?

HS: This is most especially for the sensation of the beauty and the joy of creation. Of the nucleus of love in all living things. That there is an open point of any living thing that can be connected with, that is connected down into this vein of heart-based but Source-based energy. It's the still point in anything out of which life, love arises. Also, we wanted to connect her with that so she can experience that kind of soft love all around her wherever she goes. She's been feeling disconnected often.

M: What are some ways she can tap into that connection there?

HS: Well, spending more time in nature. It's a cliche, but not just spending more time in nature but consciously opening to what she's now experienced as this portal in anything living that's around her. Plants are easy because they are rooted. They are not moving; they are patiently waiting to be tapped into. They love to share these codes, this energy, this Source point. It's part of their sacred service.

M: There is often this talk about the experiment, or the test, what is happening here on planet Earth. What was the intention of this experiment?

HS: Bringing life to the planet. The intention was to create a sphere of great biodiversity, very specified. A wide range of energies and vibrations that are more specific than many other places, than any other places. And how they can exemplify Oneness by existing in the same place together as a web of life. Again, this idea of separateness but connectedness. Specificity, but universality. The extremes, but the paradox of those extremes being the same thing. Life existing in this way and self-actualizing, self-realizing in such a place. The potential for growth of consciousness in the one is amplified with this type of experiment. And for the sake of design, the beauty of so many different things in one place is astounding.

M: I would like to know some more about this energy that came in that influenced the Earth's environment. How can we work with transmuting this energy here on the surface?

HS: One way of working into raising our vibration as representative of the core of Gaia is in re-establishing, or if it is established — deepening, a reverential relationship to the planet. Beyond simply appreciating its beauty, which is wonderful, and its creatures, but also to get deeper tuning in — anchoring into the core energetically — opening as a clear channel to radiate, as if you were a flower, this Source energy that is foundational in the core of Gaia. There are obvious habitual things around diet and environment, and these are very important. But a practice where even a small amount of time is taken each day to open from heart space as wide as possible while holding a deep anchor into the center of the Earth and broadcasting. Become a channel for pure Light. It seems small but would actually do a lot.

Gaia's Theme

The Earth Experiment was originally intended to be the creation of the Gem of the Universe, a Master Garden of diversity. From the physical forms to the subtle vibrations, Gaia is a massive record of cosmic intelligence. Hopefully, these pages will inspire you to connect more deeply with the sentience of Earth. She has much wisdom and love to share!

FOUR

The Human Experiment

My clients have described various civilizations on the Earth that have been lost in history, with whispers of their existence still held in mythological stories. A few clients describe amphibious humanoid beings that swam in the oceans who eventually came to the surface and learned to breathe air during the time of the dinosaurs. A few clients have regressed to lifetimes where they were part of a cooperative force of star nations establishing observation stations on the Earth to organize the seeding of life on the newly developing planet. Huge "arks" descended upon the Earth to drop animals into the various ecosystems that were being crafted by extraterrestrial and higher dimensional beings. Star relatives brought medicinal plants with unique frequency signatures from different star systems to plant them on the new time capsule of the universe, our shining Master Garden of Gaia. Many gardens were created within the experimental zone of Earth to see how much diversity could be introduced while maintaining harmony and balance between all biomes. Sometimes, the clients' descriptions were so outside of my understanding that I had difficulty integrating the new information into my perspective of Earth history.

While all of this is so common for me now, I had to release a lot of my judgments, programmed belief systems from my culture, and assumptions to grasp the massiveness of what was being shared with me over four years. If you are having trouble with these new ideas, I totally understand, as I, too, had to deal with cognitive dissonance and my limited perspective of reality to be able to expand with this new data. We know so little of what truly happened in Earth's billions of years of history. So many records and artifacts have been lost due to war, ignorance, colonialization, and time. To truly begin to comprehend our history, there needs to be openness to new information that contradicts the history taught to us by our cultures, religions, mainstream media, and institutions. The Indigenous peoples and the Mystery Schools hold some of the ancient lore of the Earth, yet so much has been lost, hidden, and distorted through the turning of time.

At a certain point in the seeding process, there was a decision by the

Galactic and Higher Councils to introduce an intelligent species to Earth. A variety of types of human beings with different types of gene expressions were introduced at various times in multiple "gardens" to see what types of genetics would mature well in Earth's environment. The story of Adam and Eve is just one story describing how new species are introduced. It is not the only story of "first humans." The Hebrew genetics are newer but not the first. We see now in human genetics a mixture of many genetic implantations and experiments over the many thousands of years of humanity's existence on Earth.

Many Indigenous Earth peoples speak of their connection to the stars and the Star People. Many Indigenous believe that the root of their genetic lineages, culture, and lore comes from the Star Nations. Our star families observe our experimental zone of Earth and assist in our maturation and awakening process within the limitations of Universal Law which states that they cannot directly interfere with our maturation process or override our collective free will. They can, however, bring new teachings and new ideas to help us along our path of remembrance and ascension. At certain times, human DNA was permitted by Source to be altered by different star races, for example, the Pleiadians, to help our maturation and move us into higher consciousness. The human genome has been called the "galactic cookie jar" that everyone has had their hands in over what was said to be a period of 365,000 years of human genetic experimentation. This experiment is coming to a close, and soon we will be restored to our original pure human-soul synthesis form.

The organic technology of the *christ-alline* human being, in its purest form, is meant to channel the collective consciousness of the Masters, of the Great Illumined Ones. We have the ability to be in the material universe while also being channels of the pure Light of Source. Our genetics are infused with the genetics of all the greatest races of the Cosmos. We have keys hidden within our genetics that give us the ability to access eternal life, eternal knowledge, infinite power, and eternal bliss. This has made some groups jealous and envious, and much harm has been done to humanity and to the Earth to suppress our abilities and ascension. This has all been training for us to do what we are doing NOW in this era. We have the ability to completely transmute all of the entropic shadows upon this Earth and reclaim this planet as a Planet of Light!

Transcript: Anunnaki — Nibiru

Now we start to look at the human genome experimentation upon planet Earth which begins with the introduction of the Anunnaki. The Anunnaki are space gods described by the ancient Sumerians, Akkadians, and Assyrians. Many of the "gods and goddesses" of ancient Earth are truly space beings with higher consciousness and expanded abilities. There is much fear and judgment around the Anunnaki on planet Earth and I hope to update humanity's understanding of the Anunnaki and their past and present involvement with Earth. Here is a summary of a client's session who experienced a lifetime as an Anunnaki.

When the client went to the next "appropriate scene" in an IQH session, she saw herself on a red, rusty planet that felt hot, which she internally knew was from imbalance on the planet from the collective greed and overuse of artificial intelligence which was killing the planet. The client described a sandy surface and advanced technology that was used to harvest energy from the universe and local stars. The greed of the civilization and the technology they used had overtaken their world, leaving the planet barren and stripped of resources. Not only was the atmosphere and surface of Nibiru stripped of resources but also the reserves of energy and materials from deep within the planet which caused major distortion in the organic flow and balance of life.

When she described her own form in that scene, she immediately sensed that she was inside of a robotic body, an intelligent, nanotech, smart armor around her soul essence. She later described herself as pale-skinned but that it was more etheric than it was physical. The metallic casing felt indestructible, yet she was aware that she had to sacrifice some of her trust and faith in Source to be able to use this protective armor. The armor gave her the ability to extend her life span and gave her other skills and power which she used to mine precious metals and harvest energy from the energetic grid of the planet. She described the planet as a higher density planetary body when compared to modern Earth, existing in a different bandwidth of energetic frequency.

As she looked around this dying world, I asked her if her planet had a name and she said with surprise, "Nibiru!" This higher density world has been verified in other sessions about Nibiru that say it is part of a system of celestial bodies that pass through our solar system every so many thousands of years but exists in a higher density/dimension that we cannot see with our third-density form.

She described her home as pyramidal-shaped and advanced technologically. Her home used power from the Sun and ley lines for power, as did the whole civilization. When home, she would remove her robotic layer covering her form. She described a crystalline, liquid-light substance that she would ingest for sustenance. She described the members of her family unit as emotionally independent, free from the codependent family dynamics found in humanity. There was an interdependence, no sense of ownership, as each member was considered an equally powerful creative being.

I moved her forward to the next important scene from that life and she was shown her role in the Anunnaki council at the time when the group decided to manipulate humanity.

C: *I see the council, our council, our decision to enslave humanity... (cries). Oh my God...*

M: Breathe into these emotions and breathe into these thoughts so that you can understand it, so you can express it, and describe it to me. Tell me about this decision on this council.

C: *It was like (crying)...it's life or death. It's our species or theirs. We're...at that point it wasn't...because I can look at it from the NOW perspective. I didn't...we didn't know humanity would...it would look like it does in the present time that we're in, but...*

M: So, what's being discussed amongst the council? Tell me about it.

C: *Well, we've been taking resources from Earth and it's not working to heal our atmosphere. The minerals aren't aligning with our plan the way we thought. It's not... 'cause it's not organic, the same organic elements, so we can't patch up our home. We took from Earth to patch up our home and then when we realized it wasn't going to happen, we always had Plan B to move — who wanted to move to Earth; some went to Andromeda. The ones that chose to go to Earth chose to, out of their own pain, take advantage of a less evolved species. And a way for us to fully be able to survive on Earth because we're from a different density, we had to...we had to splice, we had to share the DNA, we had to disrupt the organic evolution of the beings, the primitive beings of Earth.*

M: When you say that you're in a different density, explain that to me.

C: *Our physical form vibrates at a higher resonance, so a higher density; so, at the human eye, we can only see 30 frames per second, so if you're looking at us and we're 60 frames per second, you can't pick it up with your human eye. The density in which humans vibrate is such a lower frequency that they look solid, that you're a solid structure. We can phase through time; we can phase through dimensional walls; we can time travel — that is a higher frequency of a higher frequency being; so in order for us to dense down to...be with gravity, oxygen, and to organically survive, we have to adjust our frequency.*

M: And how do you adjust the frequency? How did you share DNA?

C: *By breeding with humans, by sharing DNA. How was DNA shared? Because I see it kind of as splicing. I don't so much see it as like an Anunnaki having sex with humans. It didn't create that way. It's very...it's such an advanced looking thing. It's like I'm seeing DNA strands. I see, it like...it looks like a syringe pulling our DNA from one being and putting it into another. So, it looks...I'm seeing it's like an injection as a medical procedure. But there is also a consciousness, it's also through the consciousness as well.*

M: And how did this sharing of DNA affect the human? What was it like before and what did it become after?

C: *Well, we like to believe we were doing them a favor because they weren't very advanced. So, by sharing our DNA was allowing the expansion of things they had never thought of, such as sourcing energy out of the ley lines. The humans were very primitive, very...you know...just focused on their grooming, their shelter, and their food. There wasn't a lot of like...thought.*

M: I understand that. And I'm wondering how this transaction was introduced to the humans. Was this a free-will choice? Was it something that was agreed upon in some way? You can see this now.

C: *I wouldn't consider it agreed. I would consider it manipulated, free-will agreement. I see just sharing the smallest amount of technology — the small amount of ease and excitement in life is easy to sell or to get a species to want more.*

M: So, there were promises made or little gifts given to sway them into wanting more?

C: *Yes and handing over power. I'm really seeing jump through time, 'cause I can see humans when they're really primitive, you know, kind of like a monkey, to having more knowledge to...then I see the advanced species of like Lemuria and how our DNA is a part of that experiment as well, so it's a really...the advancement...it's really interesting...*

M: Very good. Would you say this timeframe is before or after Lemuria?

C: Way before.

M: Very good. What do you see happening there now? What are you watching?

C: I was just observing. It's like monkeys running around and they're unknowing of anything beyond them. Which is interesting to think about, because it's taught now that there is nothing beyond humans now, so it's like that mentality has carried through in some aspects. And I'm talking about the very beginning beings before any advanced race was introduced. And I also hear that when Anunnaki were experimenting there were other experiments happening on Earth at the same time, so...

M: What kind of experiments were going on then?

C: Other species using the resources, other species, especially the Draconian species using...changing the structure of the human DNA as well. Looks like they were experimenting as well, but it almost looks like it's on the other side. Like the Anunnaki were on this side of the planet, totally different agendas.

M: Very good. And what was different between the Draconian and Anunnaki agendas?

C: We were trying to source Earth material and they were trying to source energy from human bodies, from the actual beings. So...I'm not going to say it's more twisted, but it feels like it.

M: I'm wondering why you showed the scenes from the Anunnaki today? Why was that brought forth for us?

HS: The Anunnaki are clearing their karma. So many Anunnaki are asking for forgiveness for their souls, asking to be forgiven from the human race. They have, you know they went...they started this to save their planet, then to save their species, and then it snowballed into this really dark space and the majority of the Anunnaki were there, and they are done serving the Dark and they're ready to serve the Light. They've set down their swords. They're setting down their nanotech; they're setting down their protection; they're setting down their past. They're ready to serve the Light and they've agreed to move forward with the evolution of humanity in an organic matter.

M: So wonderful. I know people are curious about what the pass-by

experience will be like, or if that will happen in our lifetime?

HS: What do you mean? The pass-by?

M: The pass-by of Nibiru.

HS: Oh. It's interesting because there is...two different stories but I see Nibiru as being already gone and there's this shadow energy of it still in place. Yes, yup. There will be a decloaking of it, so it'll...the awareness and the truth and remembrance of it will come but I don't see it as an actual physical space that can be gone to, and I don't see it as something that's going to crash into Earth or crash into the Sun, which is stuff that has been told...because there are timelines of course where that plays out, and that played out, but that's not what's playing out in this reality.

Transcript: Tall Hairy Ones Watching over Humanity

This client regressed to a lifetime of a tall, red-haired humanoid on the Earth about one-and-a-half times the size of a modern human. The being was benevolent and lived for thousands of years. The being watched humans being introduced to the area and watched humanity cycle through many needless wars. When I had the client go back to when the humans first arrived, she described a group of extraterrestrials that arrived at the planet by spacecraft.

C: I see them moving. I don't call them people because they have longer legs and shorter torsos than the people look now.

M: What do you call them, or what do they like to be called?

C: I am hearing a word that I don't want to just assume because I have heard this word before. A-nun-nak-eye [pronounced in this way] – Anunnaki.

M: Ok, very good. Well, tell me what's happening, what you notice about them. Describe everything to me.

C: Well, I see kind of like a dark blue-purple, almost shimmery, scaly-looking skin, but it's like if it moves, it can change color from different shades of blue and purple like it almost looks like it could be holographic, but there's also form to it. It's like it can be less dense and then more dense. I am not afraid of it because I am part of this land, so I am just curious.

M: Do you have any connection to these beings?

C: I place my hand up just to see, and I see it place its arm up to show that it doesn't want to threaten me.

M: And how many of these beings are there?

C: I am focusing on one but there's more behind it. I do sense some sort of ship or thing in the sky that it came from. Really, really big — way bigger than me.

M: What does it look like?

C: Like...I think it is referred to as disc-shaped, like it's circular but wider than it is tall and it's symmetrical — the top and bottom are the same, almost the same, almost the same size. But it's pretty massive, but I didn't see it at first. It's like it was just there, but then it just...now that I am paying attention to it; it is easier to see. It's all very...it's not something that you can just look at and see right away. You have to wait patiently, then you see it kind of move. And that's how you sense it and notice it because it can blend in and hide very well, but just like the beings.

M: So, what do you see these beings doing now?

C: Taking samples of the ground and plants. It looks like they are studying things. They don't look like they are here to just have fun; they look like they are working. They have business to take care of. I can't really see their faces because it blends in so well with their skin. I almost feel like it's something that they just change about themselves when they go somewhere new, almost like a protective, holographic body that they just change form into so that if they need to hide — if they need to do anything they are safe in this form, but they can change form kind of thing.

NEXT SCENE:
INTRODUCING HUMANS TO ENVIRONMENT

C: I am looking at somebody lying on the ground with dark hair, and they are unconscious. It looks more humanlike, pale skin, and this being...one of these beings are reviving it, to see how it adapts. They...everybody is curious to see if this works. It looks like a woman. Black hair, and they are...I feel like they are telepathically trying to help her wake up; they are making intentions and speaking to her telepathically to get her to start breathing. There! The mouth opened. She is still living, but they are helping her learn to breathe. Now I see her eyes open, but she doesn't see any of these beings around her. She is not looking at them; she is just looking at the bushes and the ground and the sky. It looks like she thinks she is all alone, and she is just trying to figure out where she is almost in a panic state...but she will know; she will be ok.

She tries to get to her feet and starts to back up and hide in some bushes and rock because there is a natural sense of fear coming from her, because she doesn't know where she is, and I think she just feels like she is safer to hide. It could be really...that would be really frightening to not know where you are. I feel bad for this woman.

M: Yeah. So, what happens next?

C: I still see these beings on the ground just standing there observing, but I can't see her anymore. I know she went undercover, but it looks like they are going to give her some time and leave on their ship and come back and see how she has made it. And I am not sure if she saw me. I don't think she did. But she doesn't come my way. I am aware that she's there. I don't go and try to communicate with her because I feel that would hinder her ability to take care of herself. She needs to focus on getting food and getting herself feeling safe and secure before she can nullify that fear.

NEXT SCENE: MORE HUMANS ARRIVE

C: That woman looks a lot dirtier than when they first brought her. Her hair is pretty wild and ratty and messy. She...it is almost as if when they brought her here, she was part of a test. She looked like she was well cleaned and taken care of. And then she just didn't know what to do so she's not wearing any clothes, but she did find a way to feed herself. She is cutting up a fish with a sharp stone just on the side of the water on a big rock. But she does look like she is reacting more like an animal, but I think it's because that's what she has observed, and so that is what she has learned from what is around her. But she does seem like she is a little bit on edge almost; she is always watching around her to make sure she is still safe.

M: What happens next?

C: She is eating and making sure she has food. She doesn't think about future plans; she only thinks about surviving, so she is very limited in her...I don't say limited in her quality of life because that's not fair for someone to say who knows this, but she could be experiencing more, but she only knows how to be surviving.

M: Yeah. That's understandable.

C: And she needs more; she needs to meet more people like her so they can help each other and learn and start to feel...start to feel safe and secure, and resting and relaxing.

M: So, what happens?

C: So, I do feel like these beings that brought her here are bringing just a couple more in her area. There may be more in other areas, but beyond that, I see another little boy, a man, but they don't do this near her. They do it a bit further away, so that they can meet each other naturally.

M: So, they bring another boy and a man?

C: Yeah. Now I need to focus on that part and leave her for a moment. They...they have the boy and the man together because I think they do want to see this succeed. They don't want to just...they want to see if they can manipulate how people can live. So, they don't have any heart connection to these beings, but they want to see this succeed for their own learning to study. And they do the same process where these humans can't see them. This man looks more...he doesn't look as...he looks slightly different than the woman. He looks like, I don't know the proper word, but I would say the word is Neanderthal. Like he looks more ape-like. Like a bigger mouth, bigger nostrils but still similar to the woman so that she feels that they are similar and not be afraid of each other. Then the man is still somewhat slender but just more strong. And the boy is similar to the man in appearance. They don't recognize each other...like they don't know each other, but they feel a bond that the little one can trust him. And he is just very thin, and they hope that the two will meet.

I do see them looking at each other...like they did come to meet each other, but the woman is kind of circling around him. She is trying to figure him out, but she is also careful not to...she is assessing whether it is threatening, but the man is not really afraid of her because he is slightly bigger and like most all animals, they can sense if something is going to bother them or not.

They watch each other a lot. He is watching how she is feeding herself. They can't talk to each other, but they can watch how they do things, so she's taking water from the river and cutting up her fish, and he's observing and learning from it. And she's not...she's not nice to the boy yet. Like she doesn't take on a mothering role right away, but she just kind of looks at him. But the boy isn't afraid of her. And so, they just keep watching each other and see what each other do and just become more comfortable in each other's presence and survive next to one another, but they are not hurting each other, so that is a good thing.

I see they're working together now. They sleep in the same area, and they built an upside-down L shape out of some pieces of some large branches, so there's one big branch that stands up straight and then another one tied to it. And they are using that to hang meat off of. I think to dry out the skin and stuff. I see three pieces of animal...small animal, but it seems like the skin is drying out. So, it looks like they are beginning to come up with ideas, and instead of just eating fish, now they are eating from the animals that are around them and working together to survive. That's cool that they came up with that.

I am being shown like the sun going and going and going. Like the sun's up, the sun's down. I am being shown like the passing of time. And the hair on these beings is a lot longer. They all have black hair. It just seems like this is working. This is good.

M: Is it still just the same beings, or are they multiplying at all?

C: I am still only seeing those three.

NEXT SCENE: ARCTURIAN DNA ENHANCEMENT

C: I'm seeing like a different color of blue being...a little bit shorter; it's like a light blue this time, and they are walking through forests and bush. And these beings are different than the ones...than the other beings that were here, and I think they are trying to find the humans that are here. It almost looks like a search party, like sticking their nose in other people's business. They...I am hearing like the phrase "conflict of interest." These beings want to kind of take over what the other ones started. Like they are trying to take advantage of the progress that somebody else did and they want to do; they want to see what they can do with the situation. And they...it's like stealing somebody else's ideas, stealing somebody else's work, but they want to see what they can change.

M: Where do these beings come from?

C: I am just supposed to say what pops in my head, right? Because I am hearing two words: one I am hearing — Arcturus, and Nebulae — those are the two words I am hearing. I don't want to overthink it.

M: So, these Arcturians want to... What do they want to do with the humans?

C: They want to adjust them. I am seeing like a syringe or a needle, but I think that is to make it so that they aren't aggressive or combative. And I think they are taking them on to their ship and likely giving them DNA... just a little bit of a DNA change, but not so much that it's noticeable, just to help them understand a little bit more so that they can learn things with a broader understanding.

M: How does it affect them that they are able to do that? What does this change in the DNA do to them that makes them see a broader perspective?

C: I don't think they want them to be so animalistic — not that being animals is bad, but they, I am trying to think of how to say this, because they can see where this can lead to if it is not helped. They want to shift it in a slight way so that they can form maybe some of their own thoughts in a more pure way.

Transcript: More on Nibiru and the Anunnaki

Here is another transcription from my work with the somnambulistic client named Matan whose Higher Self is one of the original Elohim creators.

M: We were told about a celestial body that might be passing the planet, and we want to know about it.

HS: Are you talking about these asteroid bodies that are passing the planet. Is that what you are talking about?

M: We are talking about Nibiru.

HS: This has come up many times. It depends on what path you are on. We must remind you that not everyone is on the same path to the same next Earth. There are many destinations playing out all at once.

M: Can you share about the Anunnaki?

HS: The Anunnaki go back to the ones who came through at a time with a purpose, a divine purpose. They are a significant group of souls. There has been much information given to many about the Anunnaki. You have heard the term "large people" or the "tall ones" as skeletons have been found of them. They are connected to the Anunnaki. This is what has been shown to people many times, but your governments and your media will not show this. They want to keep you in the dark.

M: Are the Anunnaki a benevolent race?

HS: We would like to share with you that they aren't malevolent in the way that you think. They did have malevolence towards human beings. During their time on your planet, in your millennia back towards the beginning, they came in for a purpose — that they must come in to do what they needed to do here with the assistance of humans of the planet of that time. We are seen in that time as gods, but we are just like you.

M: Some say humans were slaves to them. Is that true?

HS: There is some truth to that, yes, but not as malicious as everyone thinks. These were agreements of people that came through as humans of this planet that they would serve the "tall ones," your Anunnaki group, to help them do the things that they needed to do, that they were mining during that timeline.

M: Will the Anunnaki come back?

HS: It has been said that they will make an arrival. Yes.

M: Is that something that we need to worry about?

HS: No, you must remember that they evolve as well. So just know, let fears go pertaining to the Anunnaki. Remember it is Source, soul groups, all playing out the parts that they are guided to play out that they have agreed upon with Source. People who keep bringing up these old scenarios need to let go of their fears and let all of the past go.

Transcript: Enslavement of Humanity

Another session with Tina as her Higher Self describes the Anunnaki race and their involvement with humanity on planet Earth.

M: I would also like to know about the history of the Anunnaki in our galaxy and also with the Earth.

C: Yes, so the king that we showed her first (a king in the ancient civilization of Ur), he wasn't an Anunnaki. But he was a modern representation of the ancient Anunnaki at that time. In their culture, they believed the king was a descendant of those beings. They weren't really gods; they were just advanced beings that had different biology. So, they came down; they look different. They look like gods because the people were like, 'Whoa.' Imagine if a tribe in Papua New Guinea is seeing a helicopter or something come down; it's that kind of difference in technology. Like going from mud hut to Japanese bullet train.

M: Some people think the Anunnaki were our parents in some ways. Is there any truth to that?

C: Well, a lot of times humanity's been sort of used and abused as a slave race, as "loosh" (food for dark forces), as energy for other people. The power structure of the time was different then. The setup was...I don't know about parents; they feel more like celebrities. I don't know how to explain that. More like a celebrity. Someone who's just like you who just had a different path, but like, it seems fake. I don't know. There's something very farcical about it. But I don't know about parents, but they were definitely, when we were talking about...you know...adjusting the brainwaves that come down. They were doing that. They could do it en masse. They could hold everyone. They can hold 30,000 people's consciousness and intention because they could do that with their third eye. It's like telepathy. But they could actually send out a pulse of energy that would almost entrance, get everybody's attention, control everybody. They were almost like lemmings or if you ever see little kids watch TV. It's like that, enchanted. They could do that; they could do that to groups.

M: I've seen that happen with different public speakers and things that are able to hold people's attention that way. Hypnotizing them in a way.

C: Yes. So, imagine that, but like a thousand times more. Because imagine that it's a public speaker, but they're seventeen-feet tall and have glowing wings. And it looks like...you know...the only way you could describe it is it looks like a bird head, but that's not really what it was. You know what I mean? Like that. Yeah, because a lot of the ancient descriptions of what you see are just based on the context of the person living at the time. So, it's not necessarily an accurate description — it's not necessarily wrong; it might be a symbol for something else.

M: Yeah, for sure. Were they physical beings or energetic?

C: Yes, they were physical and energy. Yes, they were ascended beings, but they were physical. But that's what made them appear to be gods is because they had their Lightbodies and their physical bodies together, working together, and they could do things that were metaphysical. So, whether that's producing water from...they could tap the Earth with a staff and water would come out in the middle of the desert. They could use plasma, like lightning in a way they could start...they could use the lightning; they could draw the lightning out of the earth; they could draw it out. And that was very scary to the people, you know, before electricity. I mean, it can be scary now, but especially before.

Nibiru Collision Course Cancelled

There are many groups on the internet and people that are waiting for the return of Nibiru to our solar system. What I have been told is that Nibiru is more of a spaceship and not just a planet and that its orbit can be altered by its inhabitants. It has been shared that, contrary to some people's beliefs, Nibiru will not be in a collision course with Earth. What was shared with me was that humanity had seemed to have "passed the need to have a planet fly on a collision course towards Earth to get humanity to start praying to God again!" I laughed quite hard at that statement! Although, I have also heard that if people continue to generate the fear of such an event, they may create it for themselves on their personal timeline of this ascension event.

It is preferred by our galactic relatives that humanity liberates itself from the clutches of overlord/victim consciousness upon the planet and return to unity without direct extraterrestrial involvement on the surface. They are doing much from behind the scenes to assist us in this process including incarnating as humans to assist from the ground level.

At this point in our human history, we can release the old stories and see everything from a higher perspective. Everything is part of the Creator's plan for evolution. We perceive these races as negative when we observe through the lens of polarized 3D human consciousness. From a higher perspective, humanity's interaction with these races has helped us mature our collective consciousness through the experience of duality and chaos. The great majority of beings from these races have evolved to the point that they are no longer a "threat" to humanity and support humanity's ascension. It is important to emphasize that our "adversary" is not a person, an institution, or a culture. Service-to-self consciousness in a person or collective consciousness is the devouring force that causes chaos and suffering in the cosmos. As "evil" as it seems, it serves as a contrast to create conditions for exponential consciousness expansion.

There does seem to be a connection with Nibiru and what has been called the "Three Days of Darkness" where the Sun is covered by Nibiru, or some other celestial body or spacecraft, as it passes our sun. It has been described that as it does this, a rapid acceleration in DNA evolution will result, creating thousands of years of evolution in just three days. This scenario has played out in a few sessions, but I am not completely clear if this is something that everyone will experience — only certain individuals on certain timelines — or if the DNA changes will happen in another way. "They" do not want to give us the whole plan because it would be like giving the answers to our great test.

Transcript: Star Family from Sirius

I met Zoey on the beach in Thailand. We instantly had a strong connection. Meeting her was like catching up with a dear friend. After a few days, we decided to do a session with the intention of knowing what our connection was from the past. I asked for her to be shown a lifetime that she, Ron, and I were together. She had very little knowledge about extraterrestrials and really had no idea what a "starseed" was. The information she received was quite life-changing for her!

C: *It's like black matter and stars, and I can see the Moon. It's a peaceful state, but I don't know how I'm there. There is black matter and stars everywhere. It seems like it is outside in the universe. I see the Earth from the top.*

M: **How wonderful. How does she look?**

C: *She looks white and blue. It looks very icy...ice. I think we are waiting for the Earth to get flooded. The Earth will be all water. We will wait for this to happen and then go back after. We are observing from the stars and observing the Earth. But there is no time at the same time, so there are no thoughts. We are waiting, but we are not really waiting. We are just observing with no feelings. I think we are nothing. Just one with everything. The Earth is all ice and water, and what I get is this ice will melt, and it will go all water on the planet. It's going to start over again — the planet itself. So that's when we will go, to start over. We will start over from the beginning, and we're going to help in that.*

M: **What causes the ice to melt?**

C: *I see the Sun. The Sun is very close to the Earth and looks very fiery. I can see waves around the Sun going. That's what I can see.*

M: **When you said we were going to start over again, what was the Earth like before the ice?**

C: *I see it was very primal, a lot of fighting, killing, and wars. It was nothing more than this. Very close to the animal life. Yes.*

M: **Was it humans fighting?**

C: *Yes, it was humans. I think we want to bring something new. I think we want to show them something more than this. We want to connect Earth to our planet. What I get is Sirius, but I don't know if I can see it.*

M: **What do you mean by connecting with it?**

C: *The intelligence that we have already and how they can connect with the whole solar system, the whole universe, all the universes, the whole cosmos, how they can connect, and how to go away from this primal animal life and hate because that's very much suffering. I very much want to show them how to be light beings. We are light beings, and they are not, but it seems like we are going to mix with them and transform them.*

M: Tell me more about that. How will you mix with them?

C: *I see now that we are blue. It's very strange. It's like blue blood something...blue...ah! I see the feet. It's weird...it's like I can't think of any animal like this...um, dragon or something feet. Very weird. We are blue and we look like a mix of alien and...it's very strange. It seems like we can travel and that we have a machine attached to our back and we can disappear and reappear. My energy is nothing; it's like light. My body is blue, grey, these astral colors...it feels Earth, very earthy, very different than our planet. I feel the Earth is very...we don't have ground; we live in the air mostly. It's very different. Now I just touch the ground and we need to make something there. We need to start creating something there and teach these humans how they can connect with the rest.*

How can we mix with them? We have the blue blood; they have red blood. How we are going to mix it without, not in a sexual way; we're not going to have sex with them, it's in a different way. How we can help this planet. This Earth needs to be evolved and needs to align with the rest of the solar system. That's the only way to do it. Otherwise, it's going to keep destroying itself all the time. It doesn't help us because we are all connected. We need the Earth to grow on a spiritual level. This will help the rest of us to evolve even more. It actually blocks us from growing further. We've come here to help.

M: How did humanity and Earth not evolving block you from evolving?

C: *It's not really blocking...as we are all the same consciousness. First, we have to help the ones that are not so evolved as us and then we have to, in terms of expanding more, be on the same path. That's what I get.*

M: Tell me what's happening next.

C: *It's very basic fire, and they're naked. They look like monkeys, but their energy feels very primal, like food...survival, they're in survival mode. And we are not alone. There are not just three of us; there are more beings like us that came — a lot of people that came. I see myself like...I wear this jacket that looks like pyramids on the shoulders, and it's so strange.*

M: What do the pyramids on the shoulders do?

C: *It's like silver-white color. I don't understand. It's a very weird being. I can't see the face, but I feel it's good intentions, good energy. I feel the body, I have this blue body. I feel it's light. The body is like super astral and super light. How are we going to mix with these people? I can see them from above and go around, and we have to create something for them, like a religion. We will have to create something that they believe in us superior beings so they will follow what we say to them. So that's what we're going to do next — work with them, show them the Light, show them how to be infinite beings and how we are similar, and we are not at the same time. They can be like us, but we can't be like them. We're coming from a different lineage, but we want to help. We have very beautiful hearts; we come to help. We don't want to kill them or enslave them. We want to help. The women are more interesting; they look very sweet and more approachable, so I think we're going to start with the women. They look very motherly; they're most afraid of us, but they are the ones we will approach. Maybe with the babies, we will start something. Start trying with a few babies, we will mix the blood.*

M: How do you mix the blood?

C: Let's see... What I see is I'm holding a baby, and I'm passing...so the baby seems heavy and earthy on my hands. I'm putting my hands on it, and the baby becomes stars all over the baby, and the baby becomes blue light on top of the baby, and I think that's how I mix it. It kind of activates and gives the energy to the baby somehow. The baby looks different; the eyes look different. It looks like big, rounded eyes.

M: How does the baby respond?

C: Does nothing. Just stays there.

M: You say the humans can be like you, but you can't be like the humans. Why is that?

C: It's different. We're coming from a different star, Sirius. It's different. We don't have a body; we've never had a body. Humans have a body. We move into the bodies. I see myself in the Transformers movie outfit that can take me anywhere. Transforming from one place to another. I see myself in space and then going straight into sitting next to the fire with these humans. No time experience. Humans will never understand that. It's different, but that's what our purpose is, to make them like us. It's basically to make them like us, but they're not now. This is the purpose of the universe expanding, evolving.

M: So, you'll help them be more like light?

C: Yes.

Human Initiated Contact with Star Family

Humanity has been assisted since the very beginning by our extraterrestrial relatives. In fact, WE ARE EXTRATERREISTRIALS!

These advanced intelligent races have been permitted to assist us at each major junction of our development and only when we were ready. As we, as humanity, open our minds and our hearts to our cosmic and celestial lineages, we send out a signal that we are ready for the next stages of collaboration. Contact has already begun for many people through dreams, channeling, and seeing crafts in the sky. There are many people around the Earth that are initiating extraterrestrial contact to welcome in this next family reunion. I highly recommend checking out the work of Dr. Stephen Greer and his CE5 protocols for initiating contact with Star Family. The key to initiating this reunion is an open heart, loving intention, and the desire to connect!

FIVE

Lemuria and Atlantis

The first human, high-consciousness civilization on the Earth that was described through our hypnosis sessions is the ancient civilization of Lemuria, sometimes called Mu, which is commonly understood to have existed in the area of the Pacific Ocean which is now underwater. The remnants of this continent are the Hawaiian and Pacific Islands, and the Indigenous of those locations are said to be descendants of Lemuria. For some reason, not many clients regress to Lemurian lives, and we only get snippets of information. When I asked, "They" (the higher consciousness collective that guides humanity) said that humanity is not yet ready for the full story, and it will be revealed later. I will share a summary of what I understand to be true.

By the time of Lemuria, many varieties of human beings were introduced around the planet in many "gardens." In a way, Earth was a farm or laboratory to grow the perfect human that was able to be in the physical dimension but connected to higher aspects of consciousness in higher densities. This is where we see the introduction of the Adamic human form with the fully activated 12-strand DNA.

The Adamic form was a perfect biological creation for high beings of Light to incarnate, a way to experience the physical dimension. Each strand of DNA gave the human the ability to call in higher bandwidths of energetic knowing and higher consciousness access reaching all the way to Source. Superhuman abilities like manipulating the elements with intention, telepathy, telekinesis, astral projection, bilocation, stargate/merkaba transportation, and other abilities were embodied by the Adamic human. This new human was incredibly powerful and beings from other star systems and densities sought to exploit and control this new being.

Lemurian civilization revered the power of the Divine Feminine. Earth was still in its original Fourth Density form and people describe Lemuria as having a blueish tint. This could also be because of the water element which was central to the Lemurian culture and was used for healing and powering the civilization. We lived in opulence, abundance, and did not want for anything. Humanity was much more technically advanced than we are today as much was downloaded from the higher consciousness access and through relationships with other star civilizations.

Even with this "Garden of Eden" archetypal society, a shadow consciousness seeped into the Earth and human consciousness. I have had a few clients describe a dark cloud (service-to-self/fallen consciousness field) entering the Earth which began to infiltrate human consciousness. One negative influence was a meteorite that brought disease to the Earth for the first time. Yet another negative influence was other star races that brought distorted belief systems that corrupted humanity's hearts and minds.

I was told of five original races of humans living on different continents but operating as one consciousness with the Earth. Each nation was entrusted with the teachings of one of the five elements — their own piece of the elemental puzzle — to maintain the balance of the Earth. Each group started to be afflicted by these various influences and began to fall away from the initial template of perfect harmony and unity which caused the whole of the Earth to be in imbalance. This started the descent of human consciousness as humans adopted the overlord mentality similar to what was described on Nibiru but done in a more "feminine" presentation. As the imbalance accelerated, it was decided by Gaia and the Higher Realms to end the experiment which was done through cataclysm and natural disaster. Many beings went to Inner Earth, taking with them advanced technologies and sacred information which would be hidden and protected until the shadow was cleared from the Earth.

When an experiment is ended, the guardians of the experiment always save some of the experiment to be used for seeding the next. This is demonstrated in the story of Noah and the Great Flood. Noah and his family were not the only ones saved. Indigenous peoples have stories of the Great Flood and fleeing their homeland by way of water, looking for a new home as their continent sank beneath the ocean.

The Atlantean Era

The next civilization that was focused on was the lost civilization of Atlantis, which is generally connected with the Atlantic Ocean on land that used to be above sea level. Although, Atlantean and Lemurian civilizations were completely capable of travel across the globe. I imagine there were civilizations and different projects happening in many places on the planet in those times. During this time of high consciousness, we developed extremely advanced technology. Earth was a cosmic hub, with many galactic beings visiting. These visitors included extraterrestrial races that were service-to-self that aimed at suppressing consciousness to control the Earth and humanity.

During the time of Atlantis, humanity began to experiment with DNA, manipulating it and creating it outside of natural law. We began to use technology to induce states of separation consciousness and distort Earth and celestial energies. Artificial Intelligence was developed, and controlling powers suppressed human consciousness. Even with galactic and angelic support, these experiments spiraled violently out of control. All of this built up to a major cataclysm that included a massive explosion of a large tower, which was being used to limit humanity's consciousness. This sounds very similar to the story of the Tower of Babel.

Humanity spiraled rapidly down in consciousness, causing a major collapse in cellular structure and reducing our DNA from twelve active strands to only two strands of DNA, and most of humanity perished. Due to this deterioration, we descended from a much higher consciousness into a significantly lower consciousness, which we have been climbing up from for thousands of years. We lost our conscious connection to the higher realms and dimensions, wisdom from other lifetimes, and many abilities, including telepathy.

Alongside humanity's fall in consciousness, the explosions caused the planet's consciousness grid to collapse and fall from the Fourth Density into the Third Density. The Earth suffered greatly, and the water began to rise over the continent of Atlantis as the Earth started to change. When everything settled, the guardians of Earth decided to try the human experiment again and inserted human species into various timelines and began to reseed the Earth.

Transcript: Holographic Library of Atlantis

This next client named Eric went back to the ancient civilization of Atlantis into a great library of multidimensional records.

C: There is a large crystalline dome in a sphere, up into the atmosphere and it protrudes down into the ocean as well. There are also crystal chambers down into the ocean. The actual city is a three-dimensional sphere that contains higher dimensional frequencies. There are crystal pyramids and buildings and also very fine softwood, like sandalwood, structures all in and around and inside of the crystal buildings and structures. I am being led to the very center of the circle, where there is the largest pyramid that is massive and giant and holds the generators that are the key to all the energetics of the city. It powers all of the resources and holds all the information and also is a transmitter into communications with higher dimensional star systems and galaxies.

I see my body. I am wearing a purple robe with gold flame in the stitching over it. It has the fire at the waist and a flare around the cuffs of my wrists. I can see my hands, delicate, soft. I have long, red, blondish-red hair and an elongated face. I am very tall, slender body.

M: Do you feel male or female?

C: I feel like both.

M: Do you have anything else on your head or any other jewelry?

C: I have a small gold band around my forehead, it has an emblem. It looks like a half-moon with a star and two or three other smaller stars around the half-moon. It's etched in gold on my forehead. It actually feels etched into my forehead. I see gold, simple lacing around the back of my head. It feels like it's sacred somehow; you can't take it off. There is also some kind of metal, maybe it's called...or something similar... a transductive, magnetic device that amplifies my brainwaves so that I can direct energy in different ways and frequencies. Dissolving matter and bringing energy into matter, slowing down time and space, etc.

M: Very good, what are you doing here as you look around this place?

C: I am in the library, or the chamber, or the storage of intergalactic information, and I am moving into the antigravity field where I am able to float up into different mobiles. It's a very, very high, very large room. Very high ceilings. The ceilings are crystal. They absorb the sunlight and transmit it to produce the perfect temperature and space for antigravity. The books are holographic and are not read, but energetic resonance and signatures are absorbed into the system and then expanded so that the knowledge becomes immediately downloaded or uploaded or activated within the consciousness of the person who is activating the information. I am at the top. I am reading about the seeding of the human race and the cycles that they are to go through. There is complete knowledge and understanding of the imminent destruction in different cycles that we will go through in human society and the loss of all information. And diving deep there is a softness, an acceptance of it, but it is many, many millennia away. This is the height of Atlantean civilization. The height of the last Light Age. There is very little if no suffering or illness in this existence here.

M: Why don't you tell me about your reading for the time we are currently alive in.

C: It is a time where the majority of people upon the planet are imprisoned. They believe that they must struggle and fight in order to deserve a semblance of love or nourishment that already has been a birthright. The fear to release such a reality is at its highest. It's like humanity is standing at the brink of a cliff looking down and just becoming aware of their imminent peril. Just that moment of rushing toward that cliff and stopping, but not even knowing there is a huge crevasse. A canyon there. And that in those moments where everything seems to slow down, milliseconds really, when you realize I've come too far. Now there is a great divide, and I cannot go back. I cannot stop myself from falling, and I am going to fall. And the fear is the greatest that it could be. And inevitably there is a surrender as there is no way to stop themselves and the fall takes place. But when the fall happens, they simply step into another form of matter, lighter and invisible. It holds them. And the changes shall be swift, the destruction swift, the rebuilding swift. Faster than anyone can imagine. New forms are taking shape already.

M: How is this form taking shape? What is forming this?

C: Those that are awakening to the truth and their memory, and they have come to be again. Holding these literal structures in their matter and form and through their radiations, they will create a new magnetic field that activates magnets inside of people who are afraid. It calls them forth, summons them, in a way that is impossible for them to deny. They are called forth into the field. And more ideas and more brains join together in a solution; solutions begin to pour forth from the inner records that we already have and hold activated, and then everyone takes their role and place and begins to revolutionize the foundational systems of humanity. Environmental issues will be solved. The Earth, of course, will shift and change her face so the ecosystems can rebalance. This will take a lot of time; however, the memories of how to access weather control will become very swift and move so that the places that new humanities and systems are beginning to form shall be protected from the rest of the Earth's shifts and changes. The political system will be completely dead as it is known of now, and a new system of leadership shall emerge where people are much more responsible for their own inner ecosystem, which then naturally harmonizes in collective communities that can (concurrently) reach out and out in greater and greater harmonies. Resistance will still have its function, but it will be valued accordingly, and therefore pain will be experienced in much of a different way. For it is valuable only in the way that it expands awareness of their capacity to bring forth the Light that is meant to spread across the globe. In this new way, there will be many years, as it seems, of further division and deterioration and yet these new models and systems will swiftly take form. Those that resist this, and resist the magnetic pull, will be leaving the body.

M: Very good. Is there anything else in that book that is important for today?

C: The absolute knowing that there is nothing to which one can worry about.

Transcript: Mer-people, Gathering of the Tribes

The next client, Lenora, initially came into the scene as a human male who was carrying a lantern and walking down a cave-system trail deep into the Earth. She had a sense that she was going on an adventure. I suggested that she move forward on the path until she arrived at where she was going to learn and explore.

C: It's blue and luminous. There's water. I am breathing underwater.

M: You're breathing underwater? (Yeah). What do you see as you go through this water? What do you experience there?

C: Feels good to be here again.

M: Yeah. Sounds very relaxing. What do you do when you swim through this water? What is your purpose there?

C: It feels like I'm remembering, like a limitless possibilities kind of feeling. Like I'd forgotten that I can do this.

M: Must be nice to remember your limitlessness.

C: Yeah, I forgot that I could do it all alone and I forgot that at any moment when I turn the corner my friends are all still there.

M: Tell me more about that.

C: There's a whole community of people under here. We've lived here before. And there's a whole magical world under this water.

M: Describe it to me.

C: It's this really advanced place. Oh my god, the consciousness is so high. I can feel it in my cells and my buzzing. I just see this straightness in everybody. The fluidness of their body. The straightness of their vertebras. I don't even know if that's a spine. These creatures they... We are with fins too. They look like mermaids!

M: You said they have fins? *(Yeah).* **Where do they have fins?**

C: These like tail, like from their feet would be. It is like something that would help them move even more in the water. They are so beautiful and sparkly. And it's just like the creation of it is so smart for the movement, but they still have arms.

M: I want you to look down at your body and see what your body looks like now that you're there.

C: I have it too!

M: What does yours look like?

C: Oh my gosh it's so nice. It's sparkly. Everything is. Because we are underwater everything is kind of a blue tinge. Like blue shiny, elegant, thin, beyond any fish fin I have ever seen. It is like it can move in any direction. It's not limited by like, a bone or a spine or anything like that. It is like I could do anything with this fin.

M: Show me around this beautiful civilization. Take me with you and describe what you see and sense and feel.

C: Mmm. Interesting, because I am seeing and noticing that there's still gender. Like there's still the men and there's still the women. And there are still the little kids. And it is so neat because, well it's almost like this center place where I am. Where there is like a hustle and bustle of beings, people, entities, whatever we are calling [those] that are here. And it is like there's this harmony. We are like building... It is just lots of energy and movement in this part. So, I don't know where we live. Or if we just live like this, but this is what I'm seeing right now.

M: Let's go and see the place that you live when you're there. Go to the place where you live, where you rest. Tell them what you see. What do you see there?

C: Oh neat. So, there's like, woah, there's like some cave of some sort. Cave isn't really the right word, but it's like some sort of organic, natural maybe coral structure that... but it's not hard like that. It's comfortable to rest. To be there and rest. But it is not like I really need my own home. It is like we all have this big home. It is a different concept. It is just like a sweet place to rest. I am definitely a woman. I'm definitely one of these creatures, I definitely feel feminine. I definitely have this feeling that I, that I am a woman of some sort. So, we have these little nooks for resting.

M: How about the relationships of the beings that are with you? I want you to see those people that rest with you in this place. Describe them to me as you look around.

C: Like this feeling that we are actually really and truly all one being. It's really, you know when the one next to me starts to feel something like he's getting sleepy, it brings the other ones into that same feeling. So, it's like this really deep empathy that we all share. Like we are all so the same being and so connected in this way. It is also like I just feel love. The feeling is that I do not know if there is any danger.

M: What do you eat for nourishment? Do you eat anything? See yourself doing what you do now for fueling yourself, for nourishing yourself. Tell me what you see there.

C: It is almost like a prayer circle. It is like a circuit like a wheel but horizontal and we all sit on this wheel together. Maybe not all of us at the same time but maybe like eight of us or nine of us and we all sit together on this wheel contraption thing, and we just sit there, and we recharge on it like it's just like, the energy just is like a whole new wave of buzz. Oh, wow! That is really nice!

M: Allow it to recharge you. Welcome it into your body. Tell me what it is like to be recharged by this experience, what does it do?

C: Ohhhhh Wow. It is a lot of really good energy. It's like oh wow, it's like this pulse. A buzz. Warm and electrifying but stimulating but subtle. It's like the energy of the pure water that surrounds us. It is bringing us back to that exact structured state. It structures all of the water in us. It just brings us back to total perfection. That's all.

M: How blessed you are to have this supply of energy and community.

C: Wow!

M: I want you to see now what you do with most of your time. Tell me what you see. What are you doing there?

C: Seems like we are mostly always together with the others. It is like where we are wanting to figure something out together. Like we came here to learn. What we are figuring out together is how to create the highest feeling of structure between our fields. So, what we do is we swim. One of the things we are doing right now is we are swimming around each other in this pattern. It is like we are seeing how close together we can be but still have some space apart and we are feeling, we are really tuning into the energy that gets created in our collective field. So, if I am a little bit further away, I notice that I am closer to someone else on this side, and then there's someone else above me that's a little bit further away.

So, we are all weaving in this really cool way that there's like spaces in between us and we're playing with the spaces in between us to feel what harmony feels like. We know what harmony feels like and what that buzz feels like because we have those devices, we have those machines, and so those are these amazing tools that I do not even know who created those or where they came from, but this amazing device reminds us of this perfect feeling.

We are remembering how to weave with one another while we are swimming and flowing in this way so that we could actually recreate with our bodies that same exact sensation. We are getting more sensitive at the same time, and we are learning a lot this way. It feels like that is just one of the many things that we do.

M: Well, let's see what else you do. Let's move to another activity. Another scene where you're seeing what you do there. Move to that next scene and tell me what you see.

C: Okay, so besides movement that was a question I had are we always moving? Besides movement I see. I see also this like really powerful, almost like you could call it a "temple space". Yeah, this space where... Then we sit. We sit in this way. It is so interesting for this part. It doesn't really feel like we have fins anymore. Maybe we don't need them.

M: Tune into that and tell me what it's about.

C: Yeah. There's still a sense of gravity. I definitely still feel like we are on the floor of the temple and we're kneeling together. We're all facing the same direction. We're not in a circle. Some practices are facing each other and feeling the energy that way and right now we are kneeling, and we are all facing, yeah, the same kind of like "spot". We are all on this floor together. We are kneeling in this meditation. What we are doing in this meditation, well, it all feels kind of similar, right? It all feels like there is the same goal. It is like the concentration of this energy in our individual. We focus a lot on this collective and we are still in this collective. But in this collective, it's like clearing. Where all of the energy that [has been individually cultivated] gets to come back into our own spaces. Our own body. Almost like we're creating a prism. Like each of our bodies, we are creating individual prisms. Oh, I am seeing it more clearly now. Oh, when we sit down, we are creating a perfect prism with our bodies. Our physical bodies do not look like that. But that is what our energy is doing. It is creating a perfect prism. Then this prism with the individual strengthening of our individual light, we're creating this really, really... It's a rainbow! Each person has an individual color in this prism. So, this reflects upward. When we refine it more and more, when we sit for longer and get even better at our practice, the prism creates this one frequency. This one stream of light is blasting upwards. It is a powerful light that we can create together.

M: When this light travels up, where does it go?

C: Wow!

M: What do you see there?

C: Whoa. We are connecting to a different planet.

M: Tell me about this connection. What do you see there?

C: It is like this little blue planet that's surrounded by a bunch of other planets just in the middle of space. Wow! It feels so good to feel the connection with a planet that far away. It feels like, we are charging up this little cold planet. That is what it feels like.

M: So, you all combine your rainbow prism light to direct it to this planet to regenerate it in some way?

C: Yeah, exactly. We are bringing it back to life. Like it's gone cold and kind of dormant. But like, yeah, exactly.

M: What happens when you send this light to this other planet?

C: It's an alive thing, which is, it was just so nice to feel because there's this communication. When we're blasting the little planet with our prism, I'm noticing that there's a relationship. That it isn't... It's alive too, even if it's subtly alive right now. It's like it's still bringing its energy and grace and gratitude back to us and there's like this network that we're opening up between it and us so as we're blasting it with prism light it's also reflecting it back to us and strengthening our abilities. Wow!

M: That's so lovely. Why has your community decided to help this planet?

C: It is our mission. Yeah, we chose to do this.

M: Wonderful. So, you decided to help like it was time to help this planet?

C: Yeah, well, I think it's because it feels like because we've done this before to a lot of different planets. So, it's like we knew we were closer... We were the closest in the ability to harmonize and know our mission and to do this. It is kind of what we do. Yeah, it's kind of what we do. It's not just this planet. That is what our team does. We can bring these things back to life and we know how to do it. And so, yeah, that's what we're doing.

The next scenes that we looked at were of a different embodiment, a body of Light. She would take her love and wisdom to different planets and galactic systems to hold a high vibration of love and higher consciousness to assist other systems in their elevation of frequency.

WORKING WITH THE HIGHER SELF

HS: She's been wanting to know what her role is. She's been wanting to... She's been needing lately a sense of empowerment and so I felt like it would be empowering for her to know who she is. She's felt disconnected from that part of herself.

M: Why does she feel disconnected?

HS: Her infiniteness. The advancement of the soul she came in with. She has fallen into the innocent human spell and deeply forgotten that she came from the higher realms and that she serves a very large purpose and yeah that there is... That there is grace in all of this. There is no way that she could ever do wrong.

M: Thank you for sharing that with us I know she really wanted to know what her soul purpose is on this planet at this time.

HS: A beautiful innocent sweet wondering inquiry. She is here to bridge this infiniteness with this humaneness at this time on this planet. And everything she does, it's so beyond one thing or you know... She gets caught up in that sometimes of what is this one thing to practice or what is this one art form or... And it is so much more beyond that. It is bridging that infiniteness. This totally deep initiatory path with everything she does and breathes life into, onto this planet and into this body that she has been gifted and given and chosen Herself. That has been a big one for her in this lifetime. It is new for her. It is new for her to be in a physical body at all. And then flesh and blood. It is her divine path. I think what she really needs to know is that it is not a limitation in the sense that there is suffering in this. It is a chosen limitation. A limitation is not even the right word. This is her divine purpose.

This might sound more simple than anything, but the divine purpose is bringing everything she has learned and known, and embodying it into this vessel so that she can be that bringer of total harmony and peace in everything she does. To share the infinite knowledge, she knows of the interconnectivity of all life and the importance of the structure and the harmony and the grace and all of this that she is being shown today. That sole purpose is so simple and so huge at the same time, but so natural for her.

M: Where does she have a struggle with allowing that infinite beingness to come through? What gets in her way?

HS: She thinks too much. Yeah, she gets into some places that can extract her away from that connection. Then there is the opposite too. It seems like the top and bottom of her body like when she's feeling connected to the infinite, the mind can or the brain or upper chakras can kind of shut down and yeah, close off to the connection. And when she is in that total connection of the upper realms, which she came in knowing she can forget how to bring it to the Earth again, but this is what she came in to learn. This is one of the main things that she came in to learn is how to masterfully hold experience. Master that total connection.

She does have the potential to fully not come back into incarnation. There does not need to be. Even knowing that. She knew that. She knows that. So, this is her trial or initiation or her big thing to learn. It does deeply have to be with continuing to remember this soul's purpose is bringing the divine into everything and sharing it. It is not just enough to come into her and into her heart. It is to share it with the others into the world with the different beings here and to share those really high vibrations here with many, many, many, many, many beings on a very large scale.

M: She said she feels like there's a block between her upper chakras and her lower chakras.

HS: Yes. Yeah, this is one of her main inhibitions or fears is... There's fear. I noticed. I noticed this. Yeah, when I look at it in her body it looks like this sad little girl around her Solar Plexus area. And she's kind of curled up into a corner into a ball. And it is like this fear of totally allowing the vibrancy of her soul into this body. She remembers in herself, a lot of persecution and torment and suffering and rape and pillage and violence and lots of intensity in her cellular memory, around being a woman and not being able to shine her full glory and her full power, and that imprint has not fully been cleared. It's something that is inhibiting her even though she consciously can know her power and her beauty and her Grace. There's still an entity of being that is not allowing her to fully blossom and ground and root and be her full, enlightened, self-embodied.

M: And so, what does she need to learn now so that she can release that being and open up these pathways for creation? Bring her brilliance into the physical world.

HS: She needs to learn that she's doing everything exactly right. And there's never been a moment where she wasn't.

M: What's nice for her to hear, tell me more about that.

HS: Everything since her birth, to where she is now. And forever beyond, before that. Everything has been divinely guided by grace. And she has always been with me (Higher Self). She never walks alone. She cannot make a mistake. She thinks that she makes mistakes a lot. There is a judgment or self-criticism or something that limits her internally and it's just a matter of starting to paint, starting to sing, starting to speak to others about what she knows. Starting to write about what she knows. She has so many art forms that she loves and that she masters and she just yeah, it's just time to start. And I see too that there is even, there's a fear in her around even just starting.

M: What can you share with her now so that she can light that fire and get it started?

HS: What I want to share is that it is safe here now. You have made it to a place where you know, this bubble of light, you exist within. You know that you exist now in a time and a place in your level of consciousness. No matter what is going on around you that you are always safe, and you are always protected fully by the grace of God, by divinity. So, there is no actual fear. Fear was the illusion. The prosecution was the illusion. You have learned a lot from these ones, these are old lessons that we can now clear out of your system. These are old things that were traumatic to you for many lives. For much time. Or even just imprints, whether you live them or not. They are not yours. They are not yours. They were yours, maybe to grow from. Yes, we are grateful for the lessons. Those old stagnant energies and entities are not actually relevant to this lifetime anymore. So, we can, and will erase and delete those old programs. Those fears of rape, torture, and abuse. Because they do not actually exist, and cannot actually exist in the state of consciousness that you exist in. So, this feeling of being afraid of these old entities and old beings and old pathways is actually the only thing that is keeping them around. Because they cannot actually get to you anymore. You have transcended that. Once she really knows and embodies that, then she will know in her root and her womb and everything that it is safe to drop in and it is safe to feel the inspiration come through her, and it is safe to act upon that inspiration that comes through her. It is safe to share the inspiration that comes through her. Everything that she is wanting to shift in her life will heal naturally as soon as she starts to allow the immense amount of inspiration that wants to come through her to actualize on this planet.

M: Wonderful. She wanted to know about her purpose on the New Earth.

HS: It has a lot to do with the level of integrity that she was tapping into of the very specific, very aligned, very pure soul she has. And that her journey is to the purpose, the purpose is to share with others, this very specific journey, and to share with others. [She is] also to bring the clan back together. There's actually like a tribe or a clan, that she's actually reconnecting, rekindling from different star systems and bringing them together and reminding them of these Essene ways and these ancient practices that she will continue to cultivate and is remembering in herself that are very specific to her lineage. Her purpose is really this big world bridging, bringing the clan back together. It is a very specific mission, and it's not one that she's willing to get thrown off of. Even if there have been moments in her life where the compromise felt safer, easier, like this very big. Yeah, this very big purpose of educating the mystical ancient ways and bringing the children up in ways of magic and initiation and this bardic, magical way of being and knowing and eating and treating things very specifically.

M: Was there anything else you would like to share with her about the transition to the New Earth?

HS: I think what I want to share is that it won't be easy. She knows that easier isn't what allows her to grow anyway. There's always grace, and she is with her clan. With her chosen, the people she chooses to surround herself, the breadcrumbs she chose... She chooses to follow. It will be peaceful, and graceful. For many, it won't be that way. There will be a separation and consciousness split. That will happen. It is happening. And she is divinely guided and will continue to be. As she continues, there's a listening that's needed, and she's doing that. There's an alignment that's needed. She's doing that. As she is continuing with her new practices, with her old practices, with her remembering, with listening. With everything she's doing with reconnecting to nature, it's going to be just continuous. Yeah, her psychic abilities will expand. Her brain will transform into full-body intelligence along with many others. The whole entire genetics will upgrade within her cellularly and within many and within anybody who is ready for the full upgrade. It is just a matter of staying in this alignment and continuing to follow the pleasure and the joy and continuing to create and show the magic.

There is no need to fear this shift for anyone really. Everyone did choose before they incarnated if they were going to have a really tragic time, or if they were going to have a really graceful time and many are choosing... Many are going to die. Many are going to have a really struggling, suffering time. Many light beings [awakened humans] will get pulled into the darkness into the abyss of that dark energy that they may mistake for truth. There's nothing wrong with that. There's nothing scary about that. There's nothing bad about that. There's nothing evil about that. They are souls incarnated and that was what they chose to learn in this incarnation so that they could come back in the next iteration and build the New Earth with us.

So, the New Earth will exist here on this planet, with our mother Gaia, and all of her children will be here with her. It's just a matter of if it's this incarnation for them or the next. But it's soon. The amount of Light on this planet is larger than it has ever been before and the tipping point is very near, and she sees in her vision of the New Earth and in her future in this lifetime, the full iteration of that life. And so, it is the feeling of its nearness that is in her heart and also guides us to continue building in really authentic and compassionate and loving and integral ways.

M: Thank you so much for sharing. It sounds like there's going to be a continuing division of consciousness splitting off in different ways. And also, some repairs happening to the genetics. So that sounds like we'll be changing the bodies a bit, can you share more about that process?

HS: Yeah, so, those, there's an upgrade that is needed for us to sustain a higher frequency, a higher level of consciousness which is now going to be existing on the entire planet and is continuing to exist on the entire planet and will keep growing. It looks like the machine is more fine-tuned. Like the apparatus of the human body will become more and more, feels like liquid light, like plasma. Like we will be more water and more light and we will, with that, be in a more, like our all of our consciousnesses are coming together. And we are realizing and remembering that we work better and more efficiently in this deep, deep cooperation.

Our bodies will transform in the ways that they need to in order for the energetics of the energies to pass even more cleanly between each other to have the electrical impulse. The being that we are becoming as one entire human species or beyond human species. The superhuman species, this one consciousness. Our bodies will need to be more malleable; we will need to detoxify deeply.

This is why the path of the Essenes has always been very deep in this soul. The purification process of fasting and meditation and clearing our consciousness and being kind to everyone. Even getting to the point where we love everyone that we thought was evil, or we thought was an enemy, all of those things are now dissolving into the truth of us cooperating into a really cohesive, coherent structure. This has been our goal all along on this planet. This is why we came here, all of us. This has been what keeps ringing really true is that the way that we do complete this mission is by each individual, one of us, coming into ourselves so fully allowing the soul embodied in its completion, and really getting clear on what our specific tribe is. What our specific genetic frequency is, what our specific clan is, and what our specific values are. What are those specific things for each individual? Then we will know where our perfect piece is to fit into this puzzle.

That is how harmonization does and will happen when each of us stands true, and continues to stand true to those values, even when it looks like the rest of the world is going crazy or thinking the opposite of us or whatever pressures there may be. And there will be because we are very high-level advanced beings here on this planet. Every single one of us, no matter how far we fall from that in this experience, we are all very, very high-level beings in this experience. We all have the capacity to remember our core values and because of that, we all have the capacity to be completely teetered off from that and to the opposite extreme where we have no idea where we are, who we are, what our values are, and what matters to us. And so that is the pressure of the evolution that is bringing us into the fullest alignment with what is true to us.

Nobody is right or wrong in their beliefs, it's just a matter of what is deeply, deeply true. All of the false beliefs will fall away when we get truer and clearer and clear. Then we will find that we do have a very similar belief. As we do come closer and closer and closer to unity, we cannot keep eating the animal. We just cannot, they are part of the ascension process. And the ones that do, it just feels like they need to keep coming back and remembering again, that they're part of the choir, and that they're essential in this process as well. And they have an equal opportunity. We are the ones that allow these other lower consciousness beings to evolve.

M: That makes sense, yeah. I am wondering about the area that she's in and the region that she said. Can you share about the community there and the evolution of that region?

HS: There is a coming together of tribes into this part of the world. That is learning how to, on a microcosmic scale, do what we are to do on a larger scale. Where we are in the process of learning how to be one body, and how to cooperate. The fires that were experienced here, were a big catalyst to this cooperation, this willingness to help one another. This pandemic that was just experienced, was also another big opening and opportunity for people of all different kinds to come together and remember that we are all one kind and cooperate together.

There is a spark of potential that exists in this part of the world. As far as physical, and natural disasters ago, it feels very unknown, depending on how well we harmonize and remember the magic that we actually do create and the impact that we do have on the weather. Specifically, we do have the ability to make it rain. The karma of this area is asking us to come together and become more magical, to step into our abilities. Coming together, going into a deep trance, and going into meditation together as a collective, because it's not for one person to do. We can do it! We can, in this part of the world, stop this natural disaster that happens every season. We can make this a more tropical climate that is simpler and more natural and more comfortable for us all to live in without fear of something coming in to take our houses and all of this fear.

We actually are asking to embody love more, to embody our magic more and to come into harmony more, and to start doing these sacred practices together. To set up times, centers, and places where we actually remember these things together and actually take action on doing these things together. And so, there are masterful people here. And it is also just a matter of how are we going to do it? Can we do it? Are we going to do it? How much time does it take? Are we going to? Who is going to get these groups together and start making the magic happen?

SIX

Atlantean Cataclysm

Here is another section of the work with Matan that talks about the lost civilizations of Atlantis and Lemuria.

M: So, what caused the fall of Lemuria?

HS: It was a group effort; it wasn't just one. The civilization reached a point where they became so advanced that they were abusing it.

M: In what ways were they abusing it?

HS: Their power. Just like in Atlantis, the power was abused. So, when it got to a certain point, all that could happen was the fall. They were hurting the planet.

M: What civilizations were before Lemuria?

HS: There have been many.

M: Can you share with us some of what these other civilizations were like? Maybe even their names?

HS: There was a time when there were just animals on the planet and it was a beautiful garden, and then other beings brought other things from your star systems from other planets. Then there were times when your Lyrans were coming and bringing humans to this planet. If you know of the Lyrans, they are human, just like you. They are your ancestors.

R: Are the Lyrans some of the first humans on the Earth?

HS: They are one, yes. If you were to see them, you would be in awe. They are beautiful. They are not as dense as you are.

M: I've heard of some Lyrans being connected to a lion hybrid.

HS: Yes.

M: Can you tell us more about the different types of beings in the Lyran star system?

HS: There's many. There are us humans, and there are ones that do not look human like we do. We are also connected to the Pleiadian star system, as you call it, as there are many beings on that star system as well. As we are part of that star system as well.

M: So, after the Lyrans brought the human being to Earth, what kind of civilizations came next?

HS: *Other star beings started showing up, and they were curious. Ones from the Sirius star system started showing up. There were ones that were not human; they looked more like dinosaurs of your world during that time period. They were not dinosaurs in the way of being dinosaurs; they are what you call reptiles. Some of them are self-serving, and some of them are not. This is where the fall of this civilization started happening. The insert of the mixture of your races started to happen. There were once very tall beings upon your planet as well, and they started intermixing with the regular humans. Have you seen pictures in your world of the tall beings?*

R & M: Yes.

HS: *They started intermixing with the regular humans, but this was not part of the plan. They were not supposed to do this.*

R: Where did they come from?

HS: *They came from another world.*

R: Is there a name for their planet?

HS: *All that we can call it for you right now is from what you call Planet X. Are you aware of this?*

M: Yes, can you tell me more about Planet X?

HS: *There is a lot going around on your planet right now about Planet X. Prophecies about what's going to happen and when. We say to detach from that. Whatever people want to believe is what they're going to believe. There are timelines that people are on that pertain to that.*

M: Can you give us a truthful summary about this planet?

HS: *This is where your tall ones came from. They are still very much part of this world but not in the way they used to be.*

M: How are they still involved?

HS: *They can be seen in your skies. They have their own ships that they use, but they are not malicious like they once were. They once enslaved your people.*

M: So, what is the next interaction with this planet and Earth?

HS: *That is something that is still in manifestation. That is hard to tell and give you anything exact because there are so many possibilities and probabilities playing out in this moment. We don't want to misdirect you.*

Transcript: Fall of Ancient Civilizations and Master Builders

Here is a session with a client named Tina who described ancient Earth history and the rise and fall of ancient civilizations.

M: Now, what about Earth's early history? In the early civilizations? What was going on here in our...you know...pre-written history? Can you give us a summary of how that went down?

C: *Yes. So, there was much...can't tell if it's four and a half or five different starts or advance starts. By 'advanced civilization,' it is not the right word for it because maybe it's not. If you think of your society of today as being advanced, it's not the same. Just like in Orion, where the technology outpaces the consciousness. They created some unstable Earth...I don't know if they created it, but they were definitely a factor. Because the Earth reflects the humans, and the humans reflect the Earth.*

M: So, what was the first civilization? Can you share with us about that one?

C: *Yes, I see lots of large stones that are cut, really precise angles. Lots of stone buildings. It was very important to...this, this one that I'm looking at now had libraries, like information libraries. It's hard to say; they're like tablets, but they kind of look like they're glowing in a way. Or like glass. But I'm not sure why they would have glass tablets. Ok, so there are glass tablets. And there's writing on the glass tablets; they glow; the writing is kind of glowing, like an iridescent glow. And you can pull them up and look at them. And then you can take them, and you can enter them into machines as well. They're records of the universe. Some of them did come from Orion. Some of them actually have come from very, very old. They hold the keys to the information. And all of this was, you know, always it's just a test of energy. So, we're running the test, right. And what happened was the technology just outpaced their decisions to use it in a way and then the waters came. So, what happened, the waters came up. So, it just started slowly at first, but then like whole, like if you could train the ocean down. And maybe the planet was colder then? And maybe more water was in ice?*

M: Is that what you're seeing there?

C: *I'm seeing a big chunk of ice, but it's almost like it goes all the way from on the South Pole. But a lot more frozen. But it's almost like off Africa; parts of Africa are frozen, and parts of Australia are frozen.*

M: So, what caused the ice to melt?

C: *The technology got hot; they were using it to heat the water. Why were they doing that? Were they creating energy with the heat from the water?*

M: Was this civilization human or were they another species?

C: *No, they were human. They're definitely human, but it wasn't as many people as it is today. And I know we know that. The population was maybe 50,000 people total. So, a civilization is at best between 150 to 100,000 people; it is not a lot as far as what you're used to now. But working with those tablets, and it's just created some Earth changes, but if you could see underneath the ocean there's so much left even some of it was reclaimed. Some things were built here before it was really inhabited. They're not necessarily human but other types of spirits, individuals, came here to build these structures. So, the Master Builders, I don't know much about them, but they travel the universe building things, or they did; they travel many universes, these Master Builders are big. And they can build sacred geometry sites that are very ancient and very old. And then those sites can be used by many cultures over a long, long time. They could be inhabited and then just forgotten about then inhabited again, but not necessarily by the people who made them. And the second inhabitants will leave maybe more archaeological records. Their pots or whatever. So, it's hard to date how old these things are because multiple different generations or different inhabitants of different civilizations have come in and inhabited the same space.*

M: So, these Master Builders built some structures on the planet, and then eventually, the planet became inhabited? And they were able to use those structures for different things?

C: Yes. And a lot of it's still hidden; a lot of it hasn't been found, or it just sort of got covered with trees in the jungles of like Thailand or where the jungle would eat...or like Brazil, or where the jungle, the Amazon, would just sort of engulf an ancient ruin. But now, they have special cameras that can go through water and look at where ancient roads would be, or a shipwreck would be, or something like that. They can see that now. And so, there's so much that happened before, before, and before. So, there are three "befores." So, you have maybe your history up until, I don't know the civilization, like the Byzantine. You go back a little further, maybe, I don't know, 10,000 BC, I'm not sure. And then that's civilization. But then before that, there were all these parts that were forgotten about that would happen for a while, and then it kind of just decayed. They would try it again. And each time there was an intervention, but the soup just wasn't quite right. You know? The soup is right this time.

M: I'm wondering...the humans that were there when the library had these glass tablets. Were they in similar bodies to us now? Or were they different? Can you explain?

C: Their bodies were different, but they're similar in some ways. I feel like they could breathe differently, maybe through gills or something. I know that sounds weird, but they process oxygen differently. There was more oxygen on the planet; there were a lot more plants, a lot more oxygen. The air was different, the air tastes different. I would say their head, I don't know, it feels like it splits open and there's more of a higher brain coming in, higher so looks like their brain swells right there. So, their skulls are shaped differently. I would say they're kind of humanoid, but they're definitely different in some ways.

M: Let's learn a little bit more. Tell me about the civilization after this one of the libraries and the glass tablets. See those images now, those cultures, and tell me about them.

C: So, after that, it's hard to say what happened, but that culture fell. And people were back to cavemen again. I see the cavemen again. Living in caves, more "of the Earth." Like the Native Americans. They kind of all got away from that knowledge. It was totally forgotten about.

M: Just see an image of what happened to cause that shift in consciousness. You can see that image now. Tell me what you see.

C: It's hard to describe. I see water where water was not before. There was arguing about what to do about it. Not everyone has the same ideas, and the population was dwindling. Isn't that interesting? They were struggling with fertility issues, but I think that was Gaia's way of expressing it that was the end of that. First people just didn't have, or just didn't have as many children, then the procreation just didn't happen the same.

M: So, the water started to rise and what happened?

C: And the water rose. So, they were really attached to those ancient builders' structures. And so, the technology, the library with the tablets, it's full of water. And so now they couldn't get the tablets to work. I don't know what they did with them, if they tried to take them and move them and then rebuild a new machine to...I think by this point it's the end of this civilization. So, in the beginning, the tablets could be read; they didn't have to be read by a machine. But by the end, they have lost that ability.

M: Let's go back to see how they lost that ability. Back to see how they lost that.

C: They became too dependent on the technology.

M: Let's learn about what happened after humanity went into this caveman phase. How did that progress? What do you see happening there?

C: I see a lot of fighting amongst themselves. It's a lot more basic; people don't live as long. People die of accidents, like falling off a cliff or getting hit by a rock or something. Or disease. Or lack of food. That's a big one. People starve; a lot of people starved at that time. A lot of lack of food. And then what brought us out of that is that, what brought us through, was the star intervention, the star mothers that came by next would be after that. I think that would be more of the Indigenous connection with the star people, to bring us back. And so, the biology back then could only take so much...this has been an experiment that's gone on for so long because the biology changes so slowly.

But this is interesting because your biology now is doing it on its own without having to be manipulated or messed...now it's almost like when you learn to ride a bike. At first, your father's holding the back of your seat, you know, and then he lets go, and now you're pedaling. So now you're beginning to pedal on your own, which means you're creating the momentum of the Ascension. Instead of it being an external catalyst, it's an internal catalyst. It's a very good sign.

M: So, what happened after that, you know, evolution from caveman to starting to move up? What was the next evolutionary stage?

C: Well, then you sort of get into the time history that you know. But even before that...so when the technology started to outpace the consciousness, and then the waters came, and then the tablets were gone, and then we went back to cavemen and then we started reconnecting with Gaia, Earth. It was a restart to connect you, to ground you back into the planet. Ok, so that we ground you back, get you back in there, and then open up your third eye again. So, you have to make sure that you remain grounded while your third eye is open. That's part of it, it's not just to get your third eye open.

M: So, what was the civilization that had the crystals? Is it what we would consider as Atlantis or Lemuria or something different?

C: Yes, yes, you would consider it one of the Atlantis [civilizations]. There were a few that have that same...it's sort of like how when flight was given to the planet, the gift of flight that several people like the Wright brothers, and then the group in France; there were several people working on it at the same time. Or radio. Like eight people invented the radio at once. It's the same with that. Same thing. So, what was the question?

M: I'm just wondering... So, it seems like we were talking about

Atlantis and maybe haven't heard about Lemuria?

C: Right. So, the flood. The flood stories, and so there are several cultures that had that same experience, where their tech began to outpace their...Lemuria is a little different because that was a very pure start of things. That's more of the Garden of Eden story. And the Earth changes that affected the Lemurians were sort of more natural over time, where the stuff that affected the Atlanteans, they had more of a play in it. Self-induced.

M: So, what caused the shift between the Lemurian to the Atlantean timeline? There were Earth changes, but what happened?

C: So, I, from the perspective that I see, the Lemurian culture was only supposed to be for a certain time period, like, you didn't get reincarnated in that culture over and over and over and over and over again. It was like, everybody kind of went through once. Most people went through once, I would say, maybe some of the leadership was there for lifetimes, but everybody went through once, and then you carry that code into the whole planet. So, everybody's gone through Lemuria at some point, like everybody, and then, you know, everyone who's working on the Light side has gone through that type of life there because it was extremely pure. And it was connected to the star mothers up in the Pleiades, Pleiadian star mothers. And so, because you could get direct Pleiadian DNA imprinted. Every lifetime you have, you collect in your personal...your soul's record, your crystalline record, your...you know, the cave that keeps the records. It's not...it is a physical place, but it's also not a physical place. It's hard to explain, but every time you live your life, you're putting down an energetic stamp that retains on your soul that is eternal. And so, everyone who is on Earth right now had to go through Lemuria to receive that Pleiadian mother energy and that connection to the Pleiadian mother energy in order to accomplish the ascension that is happening right now. So, you had to go through Lemuria to get to now.

M: I don't know much about the civilizations before Lemuria. Do you know anything about that to share with us today?

C: It's really hard to see like the timelines of one, which one was first? I would say that, you know, Lemuria was a very ancient civilization from a long, long time ago. And then after that, then came a couple of the Atlantean stories, there were a few... So, there was one, sort of off the coast of...it's hard to say because the ocean is different now, but the Atlantic Ocean used to look very different. It used to have different islands that were bigger islands, not big like Australia, but big like the Philippines, maybe even bigger, but that type of...big enough to see. There was one that was up off the coast of Spain, maybe in that area somewhere, Africa, Spain, up high off Africa. There's one down somewhere between, off the coast of South America, kind of between, south of Florida, south of all that off there. And then there's another up towards Japan and then I feel like there's maybe one more too that was in the South Seas. That one might be the one with the tablets.

M: What about America's history because they're seeming to discover a pyramid in St. Louis, possibly a pyramid in the Grand Canyon. What were the civilizations like here on the North American continent?

C: *So, the water was in a different place before and it moved quickly. It used to move a lot faster, where things would freeze and unfreeze quicker. So, the Grand Canyon was cut quickly, it wasn't cut slowly over time. I mean, quickly, I don't mean like, in a matter of days, but I mean, for geology, geology is slow. So, for geology, it was quick, how fast the ocean was cut there. Yes, they were just like the ancient...you'll find Ancient Builder, they're going to find ancient stuff on North America. And so, they're not going to be able to explain it with the paradigm of history that they have now. It's going to look so technically advanced. It's like, they can't explain it that way. But the Native Americans used to have the history, but they've been eradicated. Their stories have been eradicated, but the history was in their stories of how the ancient pyramids on North America, and the ancient other structures, like the round, they look like sundials, but they're not. They're more like energy conductors. And they're all over too, but they haven't been found yet.*

Transcript: The Great Cataclysm of Atlantis

As the scene opens up, my client Carrie describes a society with residential pyramid structures surrounding a massive, dome-like epicenter. She is in a female body around the age of 50-years old (same as her body in her life as Carrie). She is wearing a mid-thigh-length, translucent dress, a multi-pointed star necklace touching her thymus area, and a crown made out of organic, living material. She is holding a palm-sized ankh in her left hand. Her occupation is a doctor who makes house calls. I asked her to move to the next important scene in that life.

M: What do you see there?

C: It's a tree. It's a tree I go to often. It's my dimensional transport. My name is Kasha. I use this tree for dimensional transport as I'm not a physical doctor. I do dimensional work.

M: Where do you travel?

C: This is like my parallel Earth, and so I go to the material Earth a lot. I do most of my work on the material Earth. I also do some...this seems sci-fi...do something in space. Like a satellite system or something.

M: Look around does anything else call your attention?

C: Well, as I was saying that I instantly bilocated to this space thing that's metal. It's kind of cold feeling; it's not my favorite environment, but I do a lot of work there. I do some advising. There's also some soul work.

M: Are there other entities there when you're in that space?

C: Yes. It's an intergalactic thing. Apparently, this is a place where intergalactic decisions are made.

M: Decisions about what?

C: When you ask what I do there, I see myself sitting in a large room. It's almost like I'm not part of the discussion, but I'm monitoring for integrity. So, it's not a physical doctor's work, but they call me Doctor Kasha.

M: So, Dr. Kasha, what else do you specialize in?

C: Frequency work. Frequency networks.

M: How do you do this frequency work? Tell me the processes.

C: It's telepathically in this room, so I am in this room. I am there to measure integrity, and...

M: What do you mean by integrity?

C: Whether people are coming from the heart-space or truth as they speak. For me, there is an internal alarm that goes off when the truth is not being spoken. There is a switchboard that I operate telepathically to those who are on this panel. It's connected to my monitoring system within, and it lights up for everybody — even the people speaking. It's like a way for them to monitor their own level of integrity.

M: Is there anything else within this space that's calling your attention?

C: There is a horseshoe-shaped table where this panel is talking. They're representing their leagues.

M: Is there a name for their leagues?

C: It's like their nations. It's almost like a United Nations thing but in this horseshoe-shaped...I keep wanting to say enclave. There's a golden-yellow ball that's pulsating in the middle of the horseshoe.

M: And what does this ball do?

C: It's some sort of energy source. It's Source intelligence. It's like citrine.

NEXT SCENE: GREEN PYRAMID GENE MANIPULATION

C: I keep seeing a large hand, almost representing the Hand of God. It's pointing to a tower that is outside of the society. There's a platform on the tower, and the hand keeps pointing to that as if it has something to do with potential danger. I think I'm in this lifetime in a society where it would seem futuristic to us, but it's very old. I think it's that lifetime where I did something terribly wrong. I wasn't meaning to, but there was a great deception. It has something to do with the Artificial Intelligence.

M: So, let's travel to that tower. We've now arrived at the tower.

C: Ok, I've seen this before. The tower pulsates with a light all up and down that is an odd color green. It's not the evolutionary green that we see. I would call it an alien green. It's a signal. And the platform it's on is not very big, but it seems to be red. It doesn't seem to be a light. It seems like it's a...I'm not sure what the material is. It's not wood. It's not metal, but it's red. And there's a green beam the same color as the antenna that's connecting to a huge green pyramid, same color green, off in the distance where it's receiving a signal from. And then that signal goes into the society. It's not good. It's controlling their minds.

It's keeping them from experiencing their full humanity — the senses and the free-will mind. It also creates a cage environment of the heart. It is very unpleasant, and I have a lot of trepidation going up to this tower.

M: Tell me what you're experiencing.

C: A lot of conflict. I know about this tower and about this signal, but I also know that interfering or shutting it off or interrupting the transmission would have devastating effects.

M: What do you want to do next?

C: Well, in hindsight, from my human perspective, I would do the same thing all over again. It's already been done. And that is somehow interrupting that signal, but many people die. There is a lot of blame that goes around until the truth is known, but that's not for a long, long time. The truth is not known for a LONG time.

M: Do you know the truth?

C: Well, yes. This seems crazy, even to me. So, this is a time where the human genome has been completed for a long time — thousands of years at this point. There were many, many thousands of years where the human being was learning of itself and engaging at multidimensional capacities and capabilities. So, there are really ugly-hearted beings that are not from this galaxy that have been very upset about the human genome and this new experimental being. They're not part of the twelve-dimensional splicing. They're very angry about the power of the human being. They see it as a threat. They've made many attempts to enter the Earth dimension, and they keep getting bounced off of some sort of field. I don't know how it happened, but that field became weak, and this other galactic race was able to enter. This beaming of the pyramid and the transmission towers, they were able to infiltrate the human race. From the inside.

M: How did they do that?

C: This is why Jesus had to come from the inside.

M: Very good, trust all of this. You're doing great. So, tell me more about this race. How did they affect the humans? Are they still affecting them?

C: Ok, so they somehow...this was the first group to mess with the human genome. And they were the ones that did the initial — they cut it in half first so that we were only six-dimensional beings and overlaid, somehow, they got into the human genome on the inside of the human being. I don't know how they got in some kind of tone or signal or frequency that was able to splice in. And they began influencing from inside the human genome with their own splice of dimensional influence. They could signal outside this galaxy to their home through the human being.

M: So, they used the human beings' abilities?

C: Yes.

NEXT SCENE: THE SHA

In the next scene, Carrie was shown an elevator that went down into the Earth to a subterranean community of the Sha. She described them as the original Shamans of the Earth. She described them as her "tribe" that she reported to once in a while for intelligence briefings and Lightbody upgrades. She would place a device over her head that would enhance Source energy in her subtle bodies and reconcile any distortions in her genetics from the negative AI technology and genetic splicing. She shared that the Sha are connected to Mt. Shasta and Shambhala and other sacred places and civilizations of the Earth.

NEXT SCENE: THE CATACLYSM

C: *Well, I've seen this before, and now I realize what lifetime it's connected to. I did have something to do with that; there was a team of people — scientists. They had to do with the shutting down of that transmission signal. And a lot of people did die, but now I want to say to myself, "Did they really die, or were they already dead?" as far as the human interaction. It was almost more robotic at that point because of the first big attempt at the AI becoming the human. So, there was a huge explosion. I've never been able to determine if it was just there or if it was all of the Earth, but that green light was gaseous as well. And it was almost like affecting people invisibly. It was sustaining the AI programming somehow. It feels gaseous to me, and somehow, I was involved in a covert operation with direction from the Sha. The Sha were the saving grace. They've always been the saving grace of the Earth and the Earth people. They are the keepers of the human race.*

Yeah, so the explosion threw me into the water, and when I originally had the vision, I woke up hanging onto a log. It was my first experience with those kinds of human emotions. Great grieving sadness, sobbing, sobbing, sobbing...guilt and shame, and fear. It was my first experience. And as I am hanging onto the log, I am looking back at this peninsula where society was, and it's totally on fire. The green pyramid has been destroyed. The signal is no longer active. There are many bodies floating in the water. I see a being sitting on a huge boulder. Kind of like the thinking man, but in the original vision I had years ago it was Michael the Archangel crying. And the first thing I said was, "I didn't know angels could cry." And the sword of Michael was not blue, it had lost its Light. I asked why he was weeping, and he said now the human race will suffer for eons and they will know this pain. So that vision came to me years ago and now I see what it was connected to. But I don't know; I don't feel like I died in that lifetime. I just remember that being the end result of the explosion or the attempt to disconnect from those outside beings being able to look at us all the time, and it was successful for the most part. There are still some strands of signals, very few, and they're very thin, but there is still some observation of the human race. Malevolent — it's not good.

FINAL SCENES: HUMANITY'S CYCLES OF WAR

We learned that the client was part of a covert mission initiated by the Sha to destroy the tower and stop the hijacking of human consciousness and genetics. The session continued by showing the client having multiple lifetimes as a human on the Earth. The lifetimes were a mission given to the client by the Sha to go to the surface and observe the next stages of evolution. She watched war after war and felt tremendous sadness that she felt was God's sadness for humanity and its choice to choose war again and again.

This current Ascension Event is a reconciliation process for the damage humanity and other species have done to Earth and atomic life. This is a restoration and redemption plan to right all of the shadow that has infiltrated the Earth over its billions of years of existence. The experiments are coming to a close, and a new era is beginning where humanity and Gaia will be restored to their original divine templates. You could say that it is not a "new" Earth but a restored vintage masterpiece with some enhancements!

Transcript: Star Family Assistance in Atlantis

This next client named Nicole came to me wanting to understand why she felt tremendous guilt. She used all of her skills to try to release it but could not find the origin. We had no idea this storyline was going to present itself!

When Nicole looked at her feet, she noticed that they were webbed, and she wore sandals. She could not tell if she had a particular gender or sex but definitely was not human. She wore armor made from a material not of this Earth. She had a belt around her waist and held a sword in her hand. When she saw herself from an outside perspective, she described herself as something of a reptilian-feline hybrid with green-brown scaled skin, strong bone structure, and a thin body and described the scene as having a moonlight glow.

M: What are you doing there, in this desolate place?

C: It feels like I am searching for people.

M: What happened to those people?

C: There was a lot of destruction and war. I'm just looking for people and not seeing any life. It's a very panicked feeling. I was to be strong and hold together, but I am realizing that this world as I know, it has ended. In that, it is not there any longer.

NEXT SCENE: HOME IN THAT LIFETIME

C: It's a very highly evolved civilization. I see lots of towers. It's interesting; it looks so primitive in some ways, but the feeling in my body is that I don't like being there.

M: Why don't you like being there?

C: The destruction. Knowledge is being used in a way that is destroying the civilization. People are dying. Lots of aircraft moving around. There's lots of energy; there's too much. Too much. I can see it. Where I live is a hut, and I am trying to keep the solitude in my space.

M: What is a way knowledge is being used in a harmful way? What's happening there?

C: It's so fast. It's so fast, and people are misusing what was to be used for healing in ways to advance society and turning it into a place of destruction. Energy being misused. The knowledge is being put into robotic entities and not human soul entities. They are wanting to take over this civilization and misuse the knowledge of energy.

M: So, like Artificial Intelligence is starting to take over? Starting to fight back? Is that what you're saying?

C: Yes, there are hybrid humans. Angelic beings, people are coming in trying to save this civilization by incarnating, and it is lost. I feel myself losing my people. It's very painful because there are beings without souls using power to...I am just being a seer and seeing these things and not knowing what to do but seeing that this civilization is ending.

M: When you said there are angelic beings and others incarnating to help? How does that work?

C: I can see them coming in. Streaming in, almost from different planetary systems. Different realms. Most of them are from my soul family. This is the Atlantis era. It's very dark. Very dark.

M: Let's see what else is going on. Let's see what you do with most of your time.

C: I am around a fire. The word "war" comes up. So, people come into my hut, and we talk, and the words "peace" come to mind. They ask me questions to see, as a seer. So, I mostly see, but there are times when...and we all have wings on our backs. There are times, though, when we must go out and fight. And that is not comfortable.

M: When you say that you have wings, what do they look like?

C: Big, huge wings. They are hidden. They are hidden during war, during the opposition. But within the family, these huts are very, very large, within the family the wings are exposed. It's a very bright yellow light, almost a native essence. Native American essence. Star people, star family, hybrid human.

NEXT SCENE: PYRAMID AND COUNCIL OF LIGHT

C: I'm in front of a grey pyramid; it's metal, and I'm holding my hands to it. It is probably thousands of times larger than my body. It almost looks like a receptor. There is a ball at the top of it.

M: What are you doing here at this pyramid?

C: Feeling the energy. It feels like I am trying to download information to slow down the...I just keep getting I am trying to figure out a way to slow down the energy coming into those who will do things that will harm. I'm asking for answers. I am asking what the souls are doing. The robotic souls. I get zapped. I am being almost zapped by it. It knocks me back, and it affects me in the way of feeling helpless.

M: Why would it do that? Why would this energy zap you like that?

C: I am the opposition. I am the opposition. Almost like there is a robot not wanting... There is technology overriding heart and soul. It's disheartening me as a healer and a seer. I feel helpless in that, but I have to be a leader and very strong.

M: So, what happens next?

C: I keep pacing. I go back to my hut, and I am pacing. The Council of Light is coming in, and I don't have the answers. It almost feels like we have to submit to the end of that civilization. I just keep trying, willing, in the hut — willing, maybe we can will something out of this, but there is almost this feeling of the end.

M: What does the Council think about this?

C: They look disheartened, very disheartened.

M: Who is on the Council? Do you know their names?

C: I recognize them from...they don't look like they're from the time I'm in. They have white robes, and their auras are very bright. They have wings. I keep seeing them streaming into this civilization. It's not enough.

NEXT SCENE: WORKING WITH HIGHER SELF

M: Why did this happen in this reality? Why did Atlantis go down?

HS: Because people wanted to go beyond their limits. They wanted to do things that were destructive. They were operating from a place of ego and greed, and it was numbers and the political influence. The power became the center of this place, rather than how it started, which were vibrational downloads from the stars and healing and a very, very wonderful star tribe council of seeing what could be done with energy. Then it got into the wrong hands, and many great souls incarnated to help. It couldn't be done.

M: What eventually caused the collapse of Atlantis? You can show her without it bothering her. What was it?

HS: It was an explosion. It looks like a tower. Lots of power going through, surging through, and an explosion.

M: And then what happened to everything?

HS: No vegetation, but it began to do that many years before. It was happening twenty to thirty years in advance. The vegetation was dying. It became very grey. Very grey.

M: You know, in modern times, we began to think that things changed with the crust or the waters. What happened? We can't find Atlantis anymore.

HS: No, I see it was above. It was pre-Earth. A continent that is more of a star, many different types of light beings were on this continent. It is not linear. There are remnants, but it does not feel of-the-Earth. It feels above the Earth.

M: Like a dimension?

HS: Yes, absolutely.

M: So, when this explosion happened, what happened to the people who were alive at that time?

HS: Some went back to their original planets, which was good for humanity. There were some very malevolent beings. Then others went into the angelic realm. Those in Atlantis are very, very technology savvy and hold that ancient knowledge. Nostradamus, many incarnated into different lifetimes to teach.

Most just perished or went back to their planets.

M: How did Earth manage to begin to populate again?

HS: People were birthed into different times. So, Earth showed up, and people were born into different times. Egypt. We had the Celtics. Those, many of them, had Atlantan knowledge. And so, they were put onto the Earth plane, the third dimension. Atlantis felt more ninth dimension; it's difficult to describe in a linear way. It's more of a realm, the different realms.

M: So, humanity was brought back, just in different realms within the Earth's existence?

HS: Yes. The third dimension.

M: Interesting. Where else were they put besides what would now be the UK and Egypt?

HS: Jerusalem, Southern France, Cairo, many places...yes.

Transcript: Escaping Atlantis

Here is another transcript segment from the somnambulistic client named Krissa who shared a bit about the end of the Atlantean civilization

C: Mad panic, everybody. Running. Fire from the sky.

M: What kind of fire from the sky?

C: It's like a volcano erupting. Looks like red fireballs and it also looks like it's coming from above. It's just a sickening deep crack of sound and kind of on top of a pyramid in a temple space of some kind. People are running and going crazy but I'm just numb. Like totally numb and resigned to it. Let's get it over with. I'm so sick of this. My heart's been broken, but it's almost like I've used magic to make myself not feel anything.

M: Look down at the body that you are in. Look down and describe to me what you are seeing. What do you see there?

C: A woman in long, white robes with another color, blue. My hair is in intricate different kinds of braids; it is long down my back. There is part of this temple that connects to the water. I really do healing work with the Merbeings, too.

M: Tell me about the work you do with the Merbeings.

C: Well, they would come up through the water; the temple would connect into the water, and they could come through this level, like a hole at the end of the water. There is this whole level like canals and waterways at the bottom of the temple and places they could sit partially in water and lay people in healing beds, in crystal, and I learned their ways of healing and it was a lot about sound, vocal sound, and oh my gosh, it's almost overwhelming. I'm so sad that it's gone (crying). I don't know what happened to any of them.

NEXT SCENE: THE DESTRUCTION

M: What's happening?

C: I'm really sick. There is a boat, and we are going somewhere else. I haven't had enough water, but that's not why I am sick. I could pull the frequency of water from the zero-point energy field, but my heart is broken.

M: Tell me about what happened to your heart.

C: When everything got destroyed. When it all fell down and no matter what we did, it wasn't enough to balance out the wrongs that were being done. I just put a layer around my heart so I wouldn't have to feel it, but then I didn't have the will to live anymore. Going on this boat ride I just got sicker and sicker until...

M: What was happening that was so bad? What wrongs were being done?

C: There was a perversion of the power to use sound to control people to be almost like slaves, slaves for Atlantis. And they would use these learning centers. They're really all just disgusting ways of controlling people, and it was almost like it was hypnotism of the lowest common denominator to just make them work harder and harder. Almost like an amphetamine, it would just make them work and work and work, and it was not of the heart. It was service to self. It was these people in this group and my skin would just crawl seeing some of them on the street. They were trying to use the beautiful, God-given powers and the crystals — crystal technology and sound technology. They were using it to harm people and do negative experiments. And they were hurting the Merpeople, and they were trying to make beasts, like bad beasts. And it's not, it's not natural. They were doing hybridization. And it just was so...I don't really understand how they got so much power, but they did.

M: I can see why you'd want to close your heart because it all tumbled down. That makes sense to me.

C: I let myself feel it right now. I just feel nauseous. It's so awful. So awful. I don't even know how many people died right then and there in this series and sickening cracks and explosions, and I don't even know what... I don't even know where they all came from. But I did know this. I did know that with so many wrongs, it would be made right somehow, even if it caused hurt and destruction.

M: Yeah. So, you just allowed yourself to fade away?

C: It's so sad now that I see how...without my working heart field, how quickly I just faded away and gave up in that life. And I was only powerful when I was feeling unable to feel. So, I just became a shell of a person like hardly even responsive. In shock. I was just in shock.

Transcript: Restarting the Earth Experiment

Now we will explore a session with a client named Veronica. Veronica's first scene she was regressed to was on a different planet, and she described herself as a tall and hairy being similar to Bigfoot or Sasquatch. These beings have shown up a few times in my sessions and seem to operate at a higher dimension than what humans can currently see. On the other planet, these beings lived together in caves and were benevolent. The planet was in a binary star system, and one of the suns was passing by the planet, increasing seismic activity and heat (sound familiar?). The species was preparing to make an exodus from the planet to look for another planet that would support the life of their species. (Did they come to Earth?) She was then taken to a great library (Akashic Records) and shown her angelic Lightbody form, pink in color. She was then shown another life that explains what happened after Atlantis.

Veronica was shown a gavel dropping, a decision being made to start over again. She described pyramids and a building with a ball on top of it, and everything had been covered in sand as if the deserts of the Earth tossed sand back and forth, covering the previous civilization so that only the tops of the previous structures could be seen.

NEXT SCENE: HIGH COUNCIL MEETING

C: A big light overhead. A table. A big, round table and there's a bunch of us there. Some of them are different colors, but there's a lot that look like biblical characters...like the long hair and robes and stuff. But others are like fish or dolphins and different colors, and we're all around this table. There's this big, bright light...

We're talking about all the things that have happened... There's like a...like a praying mantis sort of thing, and it's kind of upset. And it's got its arms... its elbows on the table, and it's asking us, "Now what are we going to do?" And everybody's talking. And it's like a wave of energy...like running around the table.

M: What is this group of people in charge of?

C: I want to say, creation...like different aspects of it. Different places.

M: So, what's being discussed?

C: I came back, and it was like a failure. We didn't make it work, and that was why everything was covered over. And there was a lot of sadness, too. They...it is kind of like the light overhead shines brighter, and it's like it's...saying something, but not in a voice.

M: What is it saying? You can connect with it telepathically.

C: Start anew.

M: Start anew? How would you start anew?

C: There's a place. It's green, green, green. It's got water...like the Garden of Eden, how you would imagine it...it's beautiful. It's like, start there...well, these beings don't know what to do. How to start.

M: So, let's talk about it. What's decided?

C: That light is showing us this place, and everybody's mind has this picture of this beautiful, beautiful place. And we start but it's a joint effort. Everybody's got their hands in there. Ah. It's...and there are animals, and the plants are beautiful, and then they start putting people there again. But there's something like swirling in front of the people...they can't... I don't know what it is...like energy? But they can't see it. They can't get past it, or they can't see past it.

M: What's the purpose of this swirling energy?

C: It limits them. They can't see things that they should be able to see.

M: And why was that put there?

C: It's almost like, not physically, but kind of energetically, it's almost like poking out their eyes. Like they can't see. Like it made itself into a cone and so they just live kind of like...like animals almost. They just kind of exist. They always have this cone of energy covering their face. I can't describe it. It's like a cone, but it's almost as if it was poking out their eye or something.

M: Do you have a name for this new creation you are making...this new planet?

C: I think it's the Earth, but it's like the start.

M: The very beginning?

C: Yes. Or not the very beginning because there were others before.

M: So, you're going to create a new creation there?

C: They're just...they're people, but they're so like...so blind. There's like this vortex of energy in front of them, but they just...it's like as [if] it were like a giant chakra spinning, spinning, spinning in front of them and they can't move past it. I don't know why it's there because they're...they're like animals.

M: Well, what happens next?

C: I see a light. Like two...two snakes like swirling up a post. Like the medicine symbol.

M: Caduceus.

C: Uh-huh. The two...and they're different colors. There's one...almost like browns and one that's like golds, so they're not that different. And they're like...swirling up that post...I see that...and then like...they get, the post, the cane or whatever, taps these people on the head, but they're still just like animals. Like it taps them, and that chakra thingy goes away, but they're still kind of rooting around as a pig would.

M: What caused this double serpent to tap them on the head?

C: I feel like they were too blind, and they really couldn't do anything. And they were really just like rolling around in the dirt and just eating...like rooting around. And so, it came, and it tapped them on the head. And it did take away the light cone thing...but it's...but they're still not changing very much.

M: Yeah. What happens next? Are there male and female humans there?

C: Yes. And there's just more of them. They are created. There's just more of them. They just kind of appeared...like they were just put there, fully grown.

M: Who put them there?

C: Some of these beings, but it's almost like they keep trying to fix things and they're just doing like...they're not doing the right thing. They live together...they're walking upright now, at least. They're humans. They start to leave that area and they go out into the desert again. They're just...they think they're alone.

M: They don't know that you're watching.

C: Yes. They don't know. And they're just surviving. And they make things, but they just are surviving. They don't know that even if they're doing not the best job, that somebody is helping them and somebody wants them to...they don't listen.

M: Well, what do you see happens next?

C: It just keeps growing, and they keep procreating and expanding. Civilization, I guess, is expanding. They're not the only ones. I just saw other places on the Earth that there are like these small, little groups, but they're just living and surviving.

M: Well, now I want to go back and find out what happened to the pyramids? What caused that last creation to...not work out? Let's go back to that time and tell me what happened.

C: They were... They're just not good people. They were strong. They were tall and strong, and they could do a lot of things, but they were just...their energy was just...ugly.

M: Were they human beings?

C: Yes, but like more...they were like taller and brown skin and really, really beautiful. There's one that I'm looking at. He looks like how we would think of a pharaoh. He's got this all-gold headdress on. It's a bird. They can see the energy and stuff, but they don't listen.

M: Let's learn some more about this culture.

C: They've created these pyramids, and they're huge. They're huge, and they've got crystals on the top, like shooting up at space. It's like they do it even jokingly. They put their two fingers under it and move it along but it's all mental. It's all mental. For them, it looks like they're little pyramids, like they're not that big. I don't know how big these people are, or maybe they can change their size. It looks like this pharaoh-looking person got really big, and the pyramid was like up to his knee, but then he was small again, normal again. And they...the Earth's like dry and they don't care. They're in a desert, but they can make plants and water and stuff like that. But they don't care if the Earth is dry. And then it...it all starts to go. The sand, like in an hourglass, that's how it starts moving like (makes swishing sound), but they're getting recycled, like a garbage disposal. And they're lost. They're thrown around. They're just done. They're just gone like a garbage disposal. It threw the sand all around as if nothing was as powerful. I'm watching this. I'm this pink, marble-looking angel, and I'm just watching it, and it's... they're just gone. Like the Titanic. That's what it looks like. Just getting sunk.

Pre-Matter Manifestation

There are checks and balances to this higher order of evolution. If experiments get too far out of control, the experiment is reset. I am told that the current phase of the Earth experiment will manifest as the New Earth reality as it has already occurred in the pre-matter energy fields in the higher dimensions. Now, we are watching the play out of the energy as everything falls into place for the singularity event of the solar flash. Even if it seems as though everything is in chaos, this is necessary to reconcile karma from the past to pave the way for the New Earth energies to arise. May it be so!

SEVEN

Inner Earth

Before the cataclysm of Atlantis, many intelligent beings went into the Earth for safety. These beings used cave systems and dimensional portals to take themselves deep within the Earth to build civilizations. When clients go to Inner Earth, they describe peace-loving civilizations and beings that modern humanity considers mythological. Some even say that at the core of the Earth is another sun!

There are many varieties of species living within the Earth. Some clients have described being elven beings who eat bioluminous food. Some beings occasionally come to the surface to assist humanity, but most choose to stay within the Earth, where there is no smell of pollution, war, or radiation from our technology. These beings are sending waves of love to us here on the surface as well as prayers for our remembering and healing so that we may all live together one day in peace. Many volunteers upon the Earth at this time have had or are simultaneously having lives in Inner Earth civilizations.

Transcript: Crystal Caves of Inner Earth

This next section is from a session with Krissa. Take a journey with us to Inner Earth!

C: It's a vast beautiful cave. Crystals. Some are clear. Some have a blue or purple tint to them. It's very beautiful.

M: What else is there in this vast, beautiful cave?

C: Gosh, it's dwellings. It almost looks like something between dwellings for an Ewok in Star Wars and elves from Lord of the Rings. It is built into the stone, glowing crystal garlands, and they have a sun and sunshine down there. This feels really homey and comfortable to me.

M: Look down and describe your body for me.

C: Bare white feet of a child. Soft garments. It's pretty warm under there. Flowing garment and I am holding a homemade kaleidoscope. It's actually for identifying the properties of different gems and crystals.

M: So, you use it to identify the different qualities of the crystals?

C: *Yes and decide what is this crystal. It's kind of a learning one for kids. Kind of like on the crust of Earth right now a kid could have a chemistry set that still works. But this isn't one of the really advanced ones. It's to help me learn. I'm just fairly young there.*

M: **Are you male or a female. Do you have a gender of any kind?**

C: *It's kind of hard to say.*

M: **What does your face look like? What does your upper body look like?**

C: *It's beautiful. It's masculine but very androgynous, so I think I am a male but with long black hair. My skin is almost shimmering gold and copper.*

M: **What are you doing there? What is happening?**

C: *There are a lot of tales. The older ones...Atlantis fell. A lot of work is being done to preserve the ways. They are teaching us the Law of One. The Law of One is this great governing principle that allows ultimate love and compassion with a high understanding that we are all one. That what you do to others, you really do to yourself. There are these beautiful priests and priestesses that work with crystals for healing. Maybe that's how they created our sun.*

M: **Tell us about this sun. What is it like?**

C: *It feels like it is more at the core than it is above. Warm, nourishing, allows food to grow. I only eat fruit, really. Maybe there is a grain of sorts. Vegetables, but we mainly eat fruits. That is most of our food.*

M: **Do your people call themselves anything? Do you have a name for your community?**

C: *Is it Agartha? Agartha. My father is a priest. He is so kind and loving.*

M: **Ok, tell me about your father. You said he is so sweet and so nice and that he is a priest. What kinds of things does your father do as a priest?**

C: *Oh, he is healing. There is so much shock and trauma and sadness over the loss.*

M: **Can you share with me what happened?**

C: *Yeah. I wasn't there but what they told me is that this other group was making a perversion of our powers. They were trying to get control. They were focused on material gain. They created these ways of mind control through sound, making people almost like slaves. They created beasts. chimeras, combining beasts on Earth. They only thought these existed in mythology, but they were really making them.*

M: **So, what happened?**

C: They were trying to be God. They were trying to...they were not creating in alignment with Source. They were creating out of alignment with Source. So, what happened was that the ones from the sky, the ones from the sky, the Pleiades, they saw what had happened. They helped some of us. Not me, I wasn't born yet. Helped my father and mother get to different places. We are under a great mountain. They helped them get to different places with crystals and created a massive...I can't say earthquake, flood, or explosion, but all of those things could have been the result of this. But it was this magnetic or so...I see where you call the Bermuda Triangle...why do planes and ships disappear there? There was a magnetic disturbance created and wiped everything out, but there is still a big crystal. There is a still a big crystal under water there, and you know who is working with it now?

M: Who is working with it now?

C: It's these beautiful beings, these whales and dolphins. God, humans have no idea how powerful they are and what they are doing for us. They are helping to clear it. I am showing. I wish I could show you telepathically what I am seeing. I am seeing this great pyramid crystal under the water with a big crack. This healed more and more, transmitting light codes. When it is healed, there is a great benefit to the Earth and humanity.

M: Is there a way we can help it heal today?

C: The work is already done but you can send all the positive energy and light to these whales and dolphins. They do so much for us, and we have no idea. We can send them our gratitude.

NEXT SCENE: RESURFACING PROJECT

C: Pleiadians came again. They are underground with us. They are saying that the time of contact is near. I'm afraid, somewhat afraid, but it will be. It is set. We are to come up and join the other humans on the surface. Work together. The Pleiadians have said we are working on their ascension. It's from the pulses of Light from the Great Central Sun. But also, there are so many different ships around the Earth right now. If you only knew. We are surrounded by ships. Can you see them?

M: I can feel them sometimes.

C: Yeah. They are every day working with these...I don't know the word, beautiful, beneficial extraterrestrials, angels, which really are extraterrestrial beings. There is Metatron.

M: I'm wondering what the plan is for resurfacing. Do you know what the plan is and how it is going to work?

C: Let's see. It starts with a very small amount that is already on the surface. It is showing me in your life, in this woman's life, you already know some of them. Some of our people who have been scouts. Maybe that's the word. Living on the surface. And sometime, and we don't know exactly when, the call will be given for these scouts to reveal their true nature, and then more will come upon the surface. There will be an exchange system of sorts where some will go down into Agartha and you will see how we have been living there and understand more about the crystals. This is the Atlantean...there is more than just Shasta under there. There are other places. Even Brazil. Even Bimini Islands. Other places where the crystals are held. Humans from the surface will be brought under and shown how to work with them. New technologies for healing, beyond what you ever thought possible. But it's already started. That's what you must know. You and this woman will be shown people that you interact with, that might have a special quality about them, could be one of us already.

M: Very good. Is there anything else that wants to be shared about the Pleiadian plan of resurfacing?

C: The best you can do right now is believe and hold high consciousness for planetary healing. You are doing the right things by what to eat and how to care for yourselves. You will be shown so much more really. We have your back, so to speak.

Transcript: Human Discovery of Inner Earth

Gaby came to me at a point of transition in her life. She was shown two lifetimes. The first was of Lady Guinevere in the lost civilization of Camelot. She was a mystical woman who sang to the land and spread magic and light everywhere she went. She described Sir Lancelot's sword being real and metaphorical as he was learning to retrieve the sword of truth from his own inner being. I moved her forward to the next scene and we arrived at a different lifetime in Inner Earth.

M: What do you see there?

C: Blue. Flowers. A little garden. It's hard to tell. Everything is just blue. Grass — things are shining. There's a lake. Horses. But everything is blue, it's very funny. Like fluorescent blue, not blue. I'm blue. My feet and my arms and my...everything is blue. I shine. My head shines, shining dots. Shiny stuff. No gender.

M: I want you to see the place that you live in that lifetime. What do you see there?

C: Like a sunrise, like an ocean; it's very strange. Now it's morning but I feel it's inside. I'm inside. Inside the Earth!

M: You're inside the Earth?

C: Yeah, under the Earth.

M: Do you call this place anything?

C: Yeah, it has a name. I can't pronounce it. A-S-T-H, Astharia, something like that. It has the sound THH. I see Astharia or something like that.

M: Very good, what's happening now? What do you see?

C: Butterflies, things flying in nature. And an ocean. And a sunrise. Very funky colors. It's like a rainbow sunrise. Let me see... Yeah, I feel laughter. There are other species, not only these blue ones, but it's also funny. There are big ones that are tall and there are these fairy-looking things. And there are lots — lots! And they are so happy. Everyone is happy. Everything is easy. There's not much to do but just be happy.

M: And you said the sun is coming up? How does the sun work there?

C: It goes...I was asking the same question because this is very strange. There are stars, but they look like crystals. And then the sun is like in the middle, in the water. It comes...I can't explain. I mean, it's just there.

NEXT SCENE: PRAYING FOR THE OUTSIDE

C: There is a gathering of us. We talk; we pray; we hold hands. We join.

M: What are you praying for?

C: Up. Outside. I just know it's not well, but I don't know more. I don't know much about it.

M: But you're praying for those on the outside?

C: Yeah. Someone said they don't know how to have fun! And I couldn't believe that. I...we were laughing because we couldn't understand. It's just weird. Then we pray. It's fun. It's okay. And we love them very much. Some of us wish to share, but we don't know how because they don't believe. They don't see. They don't know. They don't know how Earth works.

M: How does Earth work?

C: It's alive. It's a being. And we talk with it. We communicate with the ecosystems. We all, all of us, live. They think they're alone. They think they're very, very lonely. That makes me sad. But they're not alone — never — how can they be lonely? This is a lie. They believe lies. And they make them real. And then they can't escape because no one tells them it's a lie (laughs/cries). Someone has to tell them. And they will understand little by little. Because they can't see. If they don't believe, they can't see. You have to first believe, and then it will be revealed, and then you will see us and other stuff. Because outside there are also many beings. Outside beings will interact, but they seem like they can't see them. Humans can't...they forgot all of the beings inside of the human body. Their heads...their bodies are dirty. They're very polluted. They need to clean the body. Then they will start remembering because the truth is always there. It's calling. It's always calling like "hello," but when they clean themselves, they can hear better. And when they hear, they will see. When they change their beliefs. And then we can meet! Yes. They say we will meet them very soon. I'm so excited.

NEXT SCENE: HUMANS VISIT INNER EARTH

C: There's a big light. There are humans! Not many — not many, there's just a few. Just a few were allowed to enter because they believe. And they can see. And we share with them. They're very happy; they can't believe their eyes (laughs). It is a man and a lady. There are some guys; they look very dirty. Like a lot of beards. They came on like an expedition or something; they were walking for days. They look dirty. I think it's funny. We serve them, and they want to stay. We serve them something; they're hungry. I don't understand hungry much, but...

M: What do you eat there?

C: Light. They eat plants and berries. Sometimes I eat berries. They are nice. They said, "I knew it, I knew it." He wants to stay also because people wouldn't believe him, but he also wants to go out and tell. But they wouldn't... I think some of them went back and some of them stayed. They help now with Earth inside. But not outside, they don't believe. And it's okay. It's okay.

NEXT SCENE: FLYING OUTSIDE

C: I think I am flying.

M: What do you see as you fly?

C: Earth from outside in the cities.

M: How did you get outside?

C: I wished it.

M: What do you see as you fly around?

C: Cities and pollution. Ah, I'm just so excited. This is going to end. All of this mess, it looks very messy. Little houses and grey...it's all just going to go. These buildings and this dirtiness, it's gone. It's going to be wiped out somehow. I'm just so excited. Everything around tells me it's going to go. It has to go now. It's like there's this choir of angels, and this energy is like drums...it's chasing all of this away. It can't remain anymore. It's about to crumble. It can't hold itself anymore. Everyone is so excited. I'm just flying...I like to sing with them, because the more we sing with them, the quicker it will just crumble. Like a cookie. It's fun!

Closing Statement

Our subterranean relatives have been holding massive amounts of love and positive intentions for our awakening. When the resurfacing begins, they will share great healing technologies with us and lost knowledge. Make sure to include them in your prayers too!

EIGHT

Ancient Egypt

Our last great Golden Age was in the time of Ancient Egypt. This age can be seen as a massive evolutionary step in restoring humanity and planet Earth to its original divine intention. I was told of seven beings who visited seven locations around the world to teach for seventy-seven years to raise certain civilizations in consciousness. This was when writing was spread throughout humanity so that we could evolve to higher thinking and understand the symbolism of written language.

During this Golden Age, humanity was assisted by different beings from the stars and higher light dimensions. People gathered in the temples of Egypt to study the alchemical ascension arts from many masters who either walked upon the Earth at that time or were available in the inner planes of the initiates. Journey with us now as we unlock the mysteries of the pyramids and travel to the ancient Egyptian times of high alchemy and magic!

Transcript: The Time of the Rising

This client came to work with Ron. Immediately upon entering the first scene, Ava's intonation and accent changed. The session is full of amazingly detailed information. Every time I listen to the recorded session, I feel energy move throughout my body, activating my DNA and subtle bodies. The following transcript is just a small section of the material Ron and his client have produced. I am sharing a tiny portion of the information because I felt it was an important part of the Earth story. Ron and his client worked together several times and are working on their own book which will be released soon called *The Songs of Remembering.*

When Ava came into the scene, she saw and felt that she was being pelted by sand in a sandstorm. As the storm cleared, the pyramids of Egypt were revealed. Around her, she could see and hear people talking and animals moving about. When she looked down at her form, she began to incorporate more of this character and her intonation and pronunciation began to change. She described that she was covered in robes because she did not have a physical form, she was in Lightbody form. The robes she wore were a precaution taken because if humans saw her in her true form, they would be afraid.

Since this session, we have learned more about the "I." They are extensions of Source who watch over us, tending to our evolution and growth. They came again after the bombs were dropped on Hiroshima to get a feel on the ground level of what was happening on the Earth. They returned on February 22nd, 2017, as the next wave and stage of DNA transformations began for our ascension.

C: *It is the time of the rising. It's the time of the Light. It is the time when Heaven and Earth become one. The pyramids have been finished. They are energy vortexes. They amplify and communicate. They help us amplify the bridge so that we can ascend. So, we can bring the next iteration of human. It's time to bring Light down, so that they may evolve. For we cannot interfere, but we can bring new ideas. We can bring Light. Upgrade. It's time for the upgrade. Next level.*

R: Will you share with me the building of the pyramids, how has that been done?

C: *Well, I don't know how to describe it so that you would understand. Perhaps an analogy might work. It seems as though there is a weaving of the stories of the matrix. As I said before, there is a weaving, and there is an amplification through the group work. There is a collective consciousness of our wills that we can weave stronger. And so, we weave the matrix of Earth, and therefore, we draw the stones into existence, and we place them. It is easiest to do this in sections, for Earth is dense. Slow building, but easier in a group. We could make it all in one piece, it is possible, but there must be The Forgetting. If we built it in one single piece, not only would that take longer and much more energy for many more of us would need to combine our will, but in the future, they will not forget, because they will not be able to explain. Therefore, the pieces make it seem like it could be built by man. In the times of The Forgetting, we cannot leave symbols of The Remembering. Too much, their brains would explode. Cannot, not yet, not time now.*

R: Wonderful. You mentioned now it was the time of awakening now that the pyramids were complete?

C: *Yes, awakening to the next level but not ready for the full awakening, too much, they can remember now, but in the future, they must forget again. It is a cycle of remembering and forgetting. It goes in waves. These beings are in a time of remembering; they know something is going on, but they don't fully understand. They cannot see us; they cannot see our forms. Their brains would EXPLODE. They would not understand our form yet. Not time yet.*

R: Wonderful now "I." Describe what is happening now that the pyramids are finished.

C: We collect our will telepathically into the center deep, deep inside. And there is a stone, not stone, a material, we bring in from another dimension. We sing it into Earth now, but it will not stay. Too powerful this, not stone, material, liquid, solid light, all at the same time. Hard explain to you. It does not make sense in three dimensions.

R: Okay, what is the purpose of this material?

C: It amplifies the bridge between worlds so that the upgrade can affect larger populations, instead of the slow way of genetic implantation. Genetic code implantation takes millions of years to spread throughout the gene pool, but this method is actually much faster. We are able to open the gates between other dimensions and upgrade the DNA of multiple beings at once. It is for the shift of all humanity, for there are multiple pyramids around the Earth. We work in conjunction, all together in teams to amplify all around the planet at once.

R: So, it's amplifying the whole planet and all the beings on the planet?

C: Yes, the whole planet is being upgraded.

R: Where did the energies come from that are going into the pyramids and around the planet?

C: From the...from other dimensions, from light dimensions. This time it's a combination of Fourth, Fifth, and Sixth. It is a trifecta to work with the DNA patterning and increase a certain percentage up from before. We want to be careful.

R: So, what is happening there now?

C: People are gathering, for they sense in the time of The Remembering, there is a sense that it is happening, there is gathering, but there is also...it does...only those on the edge of remembering will come, but it will eventually affect the whole planet once they come online with the gridlines. There are gridlines around the globe, and it is like pressing the acupuncture points of a person. It is the same. Once all systems are online, then the whole system gets an upgrade. It does not matter if they come or not, but some remember, and some come.

R: So, it's about to be activated?

C: We are planning, yes, it is beginning. We are beginning the preparations. I must be here to oversee. It must be very precise. The amount of material and the amount of will entering and the amount of bridge open to other dimensions. I must calibrate with the team, in the different parts around the globe, to make sure we have an even transmission. It's extremely important that it is calibrated correctly, or else we can create explosions and earthquakes and volcanoes. We are trying to avoid that and keep stillness on the planet. It is very precise work.

R: Thank you so much for your precise work. Can you tell me about the team members, what are their names?

C: Names, not important, light beings, manifest in smaller bits, all "I," but manifest in small bits in the robes to hide their true form. It is an illusion. Not embodied this time. Not incarnated. It is One Mind, One "I" that divides and is the overseer in each of the locations around the globe.

R: How many locations are there?

C: Scanning. There are, I believe, there are thirteen. There are more that are smaller; there are thirteen major nodes and many more smaller nodes around the world to help to send out the ripples farther out into the world, especially in places where there are higher concentrations of humans. There are thirteen main nodes. There are many more smaller nodes. Not sure how to count in numbers, because many of them are quite small. Seeds really. There are the secondary nodes, and then there are the tertiary nodes, only one atom thick — infinite numbers, like grains of sand.

R: I understand, thank you for this information. Will you share with me about the thirteen main places? Where are they located on the Earth today?

C: Various locations. For example, we [now] know about the ones in Egypt and the ones in Bosnia and the ones under the ocean near Japan. There are some in what you now call Central America. There are some that are now covered in the fault lines. They have disappeared. There are some in Siberia. There used to be one in Antarctica; that one is still there. Yes. The North and South Nodes have not been discovered under the ice. It has not melted yet, so we have not found those yet. I think though they are developing new technology and are able to sense them now. They are placed randomly — not randomly, wrong word — opposite of randomly, precisely placed for balance but appearing random.

R: Very good. What is the name of the era that this awakening is happening? Is there a name for this era on the Earth?

C: It is the time when we introduce writing. When time of the mind grows to understand the written word, so we are introducing that into the consciousness beyond that of just the mystics. We have taught the ceremonial leaders about language and writing, but it is now time for the rest of the world to begin to understand the pictorial, the symbolism of language into written form.

R: I see. How long does it take to build the pyramids in Earth time?

C: In Earth time, I believe the pyramids were built by another team. I only oversaw from the other dimension. Once the pyramids were finished, I came. I offered the schematics; it is hazy, because I witnessed from other realms. I believe it took many Earth generations to build, but yet at the same time, it was almost immediate. It is very confusing to describe this, because they manifested not in the way you would think. Not like with building blocks one at a time where you are stacking them like you would a normal building in this time. It was a slow materialization of nothingness. Therefore, they were not there, and then they were all built. One atom at a time, spaced out, and then they were woven together. So, it was like a wide net at first. So, they almost sort of just appeared. But it took a long time to materialize in Earth time, but it was instantaneous. It was very quick. From my perspective.

R: Yes, I understand. Can you describe what is happening from within a pyramid?

C: The pyramids are the augmenters. They take the material, and they hold the vibration, so as the songs of the materials are growing brighter in the Light, then they need a container so that they do not EXPLODE. We must match the density of Earth with the density of the other dimension. Therefore, it is like a translator. So, they are the translator for the transmission — you might call them something like a radio wave, but not radio wave, it is a light transmission.

So, therefore, the pyramids are like the...what do you call those, collectors, those energy collectors from the large arrays that focus the waves in order to send them far out into space. It is a similar concept, except the opposite, in where the energy must be matched. The large vibration of the ascension energy must be matched with the Earth dimension density. Therefore, it is a net that is weaving third-dimension reality (3D dimensionality) with the larger dimensional light frequencies so that it can be a bridge. So, therefore it is like the transmitter, the augmenter, and the bridge holder. It is like the bolts that hold the bridge into the Earth.

And it also connects the bridge into the sky. So, it is an energetic transmission network center, and it also holds the material and allows that material that is not used to be held in the third dimension. It gives it a chance to breathe, so it has certain portals to allow the energy to move throughout the pyramid so that it does not EXPLODE. There is an opportunity to experiment with the pathways to see if we can find a more efficient way of working with this material in the third dimension. As this is always an experiment that is developing and growing over time, we are always exploring how to better and more efficiently work these grids. For this does seem to be a lot of work to create this augmentation system, and therefore, we are trying to create a more efficient pattern.

However, this strangely simple and complex idea is the best idea our team has come up with in order to amplify the awareness mentality of the entire planet without causing any major explosions. So, it is both a grounding rod and an amplifier. It is all sorts of things all at once and difficult to describe to you in the third dimension.

Transcript: Building of the Pyramid and the Original Alchemist

This next client named Michaela came to me at the beginning of my years of doing quantum healing hypnosis. I had the pleasure of working with her three times. On the second meeting, we were both surprised by her arriving at the top of the Great Pyramid surrounded by many advanced spiritual beings for the placing of the capstone. We were taken through a montage of scenes showing what occurred in the pyramids, the function of the capstone, and how its magical, alchemical technology was removed for safekeeping for when New Earth was fully realized and activated. Somehow, the recording did not record. I lost the whole transmission. You can probably understand how shocked and heartbroken I was. A year or so later, we met up again to re-explore that lifetime to get more of the story for the book. Here is what we discovered!

M: All right. What do you see there? What are the first impressions that come to mind?

C: It's the pyramid. It's a large pyramid and I can see it surrounded by just lots of green trees, river. It's not like a desert. It's like all green and lush. They're huge.

And it's showing me the top of the pyramid.

M: What do you see when you look at the top of the pyramid?

C: It's like a separate piece. It's like a tip of the pyramid, but it houses like a large egg-shaped crystal. It seems to change color. I see it white and then emerald and then like a rose, very yellow.

M: So, the top of the pyramid is crystalline and has different colors shining from it?

C: Just the crystal. Yeah. And then it's like the tip of the pyramid is kind of like opal-like looking...sheen to the bricks like they're so polished. It's like a cap. It's a cap that houses stone. The Philosopher's Stone.

M: So, what does this stone do?

C: Many things, that's why it has different colors. Those different colors are like just the different energies and then they're funneled and used for different purposes. Like healing, knowledge, time travel.

M: Become aware of yourself. What do you see when you look at yourself?

C: They are man's feet in sandals like open-toed, leather sandals; robes of a brownish-burgundy color; robes with long sleeves, many pockets, many pockets in the sleeves. I am like the original alchemist (Thoth).

M: Are you carrying anything or holding anything?

C: A staff. A staff — wood, polished, not fossilized but maybe petrified? Yeah. And it's been through some kind of process, and it's alive somehow. It has a consciousness, this staff, because of a process, an alchemy process that I put it through. So, it's imbued with consciousness power connected to my own. Yeah, it's like a caduceus with a crystal, and when you stamp it on the floor...I see myself holding it and bringing it down, like Lord of the Rings, you know, the great wizard, when he stamps down the staff and says, "You shall not pass." It has that kind of feeling to it. You could stamp it down and the ground would shake. You know, it would clear out energies, clears out lower frequency or unwanted, you know, negative entities or energies. It's like a blast, you know? It's something you see in a movie. That's how they experience it, like if a bomb went off and you had the air rushing at you, it just clears it out like a bomb.

M: Yeah, sounds very powerful. You said you had a bunch of pockets in your sleeves. What was in those pockets?

C: Um, oh, alchemical elements. Tools. So almost like where you'd get the idea of Merlin the magician. It's tied to that archetype as well. See, the original alchemist is not a magician, per se. They have an understanding of the archetypal properties of elements. It's a spiritual amalgamation; it's not a physical process. They use physical elements, but it's a spiritual understanding of the archetype of frequencies of these elements. And you understand the natural laws of their processes with each other. Those processes you take within yourself in a spiritual way, which can be named as the amalgamation of mercury with sulfur to create salts. Crystallization. This is the spiritual process that we are capable of interpreting. It sets us above all, many, above the animals; the gift to mankind is the ability to understand these concepts and with understanding and spiritual knowing it can create enlightenment and crystallization.

M: Makes sense. Thank you. What are you doing there at the pyramid?

C: I'm a curator.

M: Tell me more about the curation process. What are you curating?

C: There's many objects of spiritual technology. Artifacts, ancient tools passed down from the Old Ones. I know everything about these. I keep them safe, keep the knowledge. I also search to increase the collection and add to it.

M: That make sense. When you're saying, the "Old Ones," describe them to me. Who are the Old Ones?

C: The original angels. The Nine. The original bringers of Light. They brought knowledge to this planet.

M: Good. Have you ever got to meet them?

C: Hundreds and thousands, eons...original architects. I have a kinship to them. So, there is as you say, know them, like as your soul knows, but to say meet them — not in the current state from which I'm speaking.

NEXT SCENE: MOVING BACK IN TIME

C: I'm a young boy, seven-years old. Dark hair; dark, dark brown eyes; skinny arms; skinny legs; happy, healthy.

M: What's happening there? What are you doing?

C: The priests have come. I have shown evidence of reincarnation. I am able to remember who I am. So, they have come to visit with me and speak with me. They perform these tests, but they know they don't even need to do the tests; it's so obvious. I don't speak to them like a seven-year-old boy would. I can tell them who I am and am already so full of knowledge.

M: What kinds of things do you share with them about who you are? What kind of tests do they do?

C: There are objects. A feather, some kind of like silver-engraved tool. Choosing my possessions from previous incarnations. Some of their items are misrepresented, as in not what they believe or were told that they were. So, I correct them on the origins of the objects that they perceived to be belonging to the past incarnation. Some were correct and some weren't. I was a great teacher...and I keep seeing the Emerald Tablets.

M: Tell me what you see.

C: Green stone and a chisel in my hand. I can hear it again, like almost feel it, tap tap.

M: So, they're testing you to see if you can get these things correctly. It sounds like you're passing?

C: Yes, putting them to shame. Well, I must leave my family now, which is hard for my mother. I must be like almost something for her that I am not, as in a small child. Because I am but I am not. But for a mother, no matter how much a child grows they are always a small child. So, the empathy and compassion I feel for my mother and the loss that she will experience, I do feel sad. But I am not reacting in a way that a normal seven-year-old boy would be leaving his family because it's just something I've always known I would do. I don't have the same tumultuous emotions. So, I sort of have to play a bit the part for my grieving mother, to be that boy for her, but now it is time to go.

NEXT SCENE: COMING INTO MANHOOD

C: I am thirteen. They are crowning me, but not like royalty. Well, that's hard to say. It's hard to stop other people from idolizing, which is the difficult thing.

M: What's happening on this ceremony day?

C: They're placing a golden, embroidered cloth around me, around my neck, the slim piece, not a full cloak. I have robes and then they're placing this strip of embroidered, gold cloth, like a golden garland crown.

M: You said they're idolizing you. Why is that?

C: Not all of them. There, man is just prone to, you know, to idolize that which they wish to be.

M: Why did they want to be you? What makes you so special?

C: *My abilities, my demonstrations of knowledge and power in one, so young to just be born that way. I can move objects. I can perform miracles. It's just that I have an understanding of the natural laws of this universe into a spiritual level. I have DNA that is fully activated, like Mozart, born a small child and just playing the way he did with perfection, effortlessly. How does that make people feel? They feel many ways about it. The movie Amadeus gives a good depiction of worship and envy.*

M: **So why are they crowning you now? What is the ceremony commemorating?**

C: *Manhood. The full embodiment of my higher self. They make much ado about nothing. But I am still young, so I let them perform their rituals; I'm still learning. They want to put me on a pedestal and there are many years that I spent getting back down off that pedestal they keep trying to put me on, to keep trying to teach that what is within me is within all.*

M: **That makes sense. What do they call you there? To hear your name. Someone will yell it out now.**

C: *Ishmael. Which is funny; it's like Michaela, Ishmael, which is similar to the Michael energy that we share as well (referring to me, the facilitator). You see we are many things. We are many archetypal energies, wonderful combinations and equations. So, even in those past realities, I had an understanding of my own adaptability. I am many things; I am all things; and yes, I had a clear recollection of the source of my archetypes, that is all...simply, that I could remember. We all contain this. So, I would keep trying to teach the humble principles of the alchemy.*

NEXT SCENE: PLANNING THE PYRAMID

C: *I was the architect of the pyramid. I am back now to where we started.*

M: **Tell me about what you're learning about the architect.**

C: *I see me drawing out all the plans, the numbers, the equations, and on how I knew these things. Yes, yes. I wasn't just working with humans. After thirteen, that ceremony, they came for me in the ships just like a sun, a ship like a sun. And that was why it was so silly, their little tests, because they had already come for me. They were just performing rituals for themselves. So I went; I went with them for a time, for many years, and went through spiritual training, changed form somewhat, and then came back to construct the pyramids.*

M: And so, when you say you went with them, who's them? And see them and describe it to me.

C: I just see light. Beings of light, ships of light, colored light. They're fractal-like forms and patterns. They're like angels, higher dimensional beings.

M: And they took you on this ship with them? Where did they take you?

C: Through the Sun. Home. Arcturus, they say.

M: What kind of training do they do with you there?

C: It's hard to explain…kind of understanding how reality is formed. Working in different dimensions. I'm just seeing a lot of patterns, like sacred geometry. I'm seeing like all these equations, like color-coded bars. It's hard to conceptualize in this reality the way because it was like another dimension of learning, and so, it's outside of time. I just see this rapid experience of building; it's trying to show me so many things at once. It's like it's showing me Legos as a kid, I don't know. And then these like, it's showing me the sketch doodle thing I had when I was a kid (current life). Where it's like the circle and you put your pen in, it forms the geometric patterns, you loop around and around (Spirograph). Yeah, creates all these circles. Do you know what I mean?

M: You were saying that you also changed form while you were there. Tell me about that process.

C: It's a crystallization to the DNA. Much of what we are expecting to experience with the DNA activation happening now on the Earth.

M: Like is going to happen in this life?

C: Yeah, well, not for all, but yes, that is the goal, this activation to the next level of evolution.

M: So, when you came back, what did you do? Be there now, tell me what you see happening.

C: Moving these just massive, massive stones like just in the air, forming them and placing them. Everything has this like sheen to it.

M: Does anyone assist you with this?

C: There's like a ship, a light ship above, and I feel like they are like amping up my powers, you know, like I'm a conduit. They're definitely adding a lot of power to perform such a massive task. It's a lot, it can be a lot of work to do one of these huge bricks, right? Never mind doing a whole pyramid. So, they help focus energy, staying in a certain state, they just magnify all that, amp it up.

M: So, the pyramid is being built, did they share with you the intention of this pyramid? Who gave you the idea to build it?

C: The ones who came from me, the angels, the original angels.

M: What is the purpose of the pyramid? Why did they have you build it?

C: A magnifier to teach, to heal, to set the journey. It's a huge source of power. It lifts the frequency of the planet. It makes it easier for those who don't have my abilities to like, pierce that veil. It puts them in a higher state. It makes it easier for everybody else to learn and do.

M: That makes sense.

C: So, it heals, it teaches, gives love, allows for communication, purification. There is a massive amount of knowledge in the crystal. It's like the natural laws. All of them. All of them are clear cut in this crystal, haven't been messed with, haven't been inverted or bogged down with dogma. Just the clear-cut, simplistic truth to every last detail, the natural laws and elements of this universe.

M: Before we were allowed to see the ceremony of when this whole thing was completed, I'd like for you to go to that ceremony now. Describe to me what's happening there. Be there now and tell me.

C: A large crowd all gathered around, thousands. Colorful, colorful material all around, just flags blowing in the wind. Many priests as it's being lowered into place, just the crystal. It's all open at the top. And we're setting the crystal in place, like into its housing, and then lowering. We all leave the top and the capstone is lowered and placed. And cheering all around, applause, celebration. A beam, a beam of light purple — light, vibrant purple, from the top up to the sky. I feel like it goes all the way through, down through the crystal, down into the pyramid. Deep down.

M: So now that this capstone has been placed there on the top, what will this do now?

C: Well, you can feel, it's like the air is thick like rose water. Like it's this energy, I'm trying to compare it to like water that's like silk that smells like roses. The air has this thickness to it, like this sensual, just love, and like gliding through, you know, a pool of bliss. The air is thick with it. It almost has like a rose-purply-rosy color to everything, the Light. Rose-colored glasses. I just want to say, like seeing through rose-colored glasses.

NEXT SCENE: EXITING THAT LIFE

C: I'm watching my funeral.

M: What happens, how did you pass?

C: I chose when to leave my body. I feel like I lived a few hundred years, and I was done. My body does not look that old though. I didn't really age. And I'm just like floating above watching everybody go through the rituals.

M: And from that perspective, you can understand the purpose and the meaning of that life.

C: Well, it was to leave a record behind. Leaving a record behind and setting in place aspects for the storyline. Markers, nodes in time. It's part of what I learned. We work through time; we leave points that require a conclusion. Like points in the plot of a story. We participate in building it, but it was also leaving records and teachings behind not just for that time. [for future timelines that we would incarnate and continue using the tools and sacred knowledge.]

M: So, what is the storyline of Earth from that spiritual perspective? What is the storyline for Earth and humanity?

C: Ascension always. Elevation. Always growth, expansion, enlightenment. Always higher, higher, higher. It never stops. The torus, always evolving. It's just turning itself inside out once again.

M: So, in modern times the capstone is not there. Can you show her? What happened to the capstone?

C: Stolen.

M: Tell me about it. What do you see happening?

C: But they didn't get the crystal because I took it away. Well, this was what we talked about before. When they came there was a big rush; they're coming; they're coming; we are not protected. Because living in this peace and love [believing] "No, people don't steal; they don't hurt; they don't take; they give." We are not a society that is in defense of itself, and unfortunately, there has been an erosion. They did leave, these higher beings, and it has left us open. They're coming to take what is ours and to use our power for their own.

M: Who are these higher beings?

C: Anunnaki. There's good and bad Anunnaki, polarities and everything. So, these are ones still working within hierarchal dominance; they want man to fuel and feed them. They are not looking to fuel and feed man; those are the polarities. One side wants man to ascend and to grow and release; receive; experience their full, true capacity. The other wants to harness it for themselves. So, we are removing your Christos [the consciousness technology of the Great Pyramid]. It is time; it is part of the story. And going in a large, like box or chest, gold, but actually very little adornment. It's kept very humble. I have come back to take it away. Confusing, well, it's confusing because, you know, I die, but I didn't really die. And I left, but I came back and took form, basically took form as my old self to retrieve it.

M: And how did you do that? How are you able to take form? Let's see the process now.

C: You create a template. Understanding the geometry, sacred geometry, you create a template and then you attract protons, like magnetics. It adheres to the template that you create. I'm explaining this very simply, just kind of showing, like magnetic slivers. They're showing me like if you were to draw a symbol like you know, the Metatron's cube or sacred geometry, and then you magnetize particles, the building blocks of life, they get stuck to it. And then they just build. You just take form. You can take any form you want if you understand the templates and how to draw them, and then you just magnetize them, and then it takes form. You could literally make anything in the palm of your hand if you have this knowledge.

Transcript: The Life of Goddess Isis

This next session is with a client named Nicole. When Nicole came into the scene, she described a beautiful clay and rock temple filled with radiant sunlight. Many people were around being creative, and music played in the background. I had her look down at her body and describe what she saw.

C: Wearing beautiful, golden sandals, white robe, beautiful necklace...beautiful necklace and symmetrical jewelry, gold jewelry on each wrist...showing the divine feminine and masculine inflow. Symmetry is very important. Then going up, wearing crystals, gold necklace with crystals, blue malachite. There is some obsidian and a red stone. Just a very comfortable garment.

M: What about on your head? Do you have anything there?

C: Yes. It is a sphere, but what it does is emit energy so that others can download the energy that is in the sphere and feel that beautiful healing. It's a headpiece, and it was put there by Thoth...Tehuti. He and I work a lot together in downloading and receiving energy. It is representative of life, the life force and inner journey, a mirror. He infused the headpiece before he put it on. I have women also who helped me put it on, but he infused it with a mechanism that can enlighten and awaken others faster than the use of hands. So, it's a downloading, teacher sphere. It is a very heavy piece, but I like to have my crown covered, my crown chakra. It is a very, very sacred space, and I like to receive directly from the Divine so no energies coming in other than that of the Divine and so the headpiece is a purifier of energy coming in, as well.

M: Wonderful. Do you have anything in your hands or in your arms?

C: Yes, I have a golden staff sphere and a top that has a beautiful bird...just the head of a bird, but a beautiful bird. There are a lot of wonderful energies that come from that totem.

M: How did you get something like this?

C: I was gifted, as I was a child.

M: Were you aware of its lineage? Where does it come from?

C: My mother. That my mother also symbolizes, is a symbol of a white heron. That being at the top of the staff was very important.

NEXT SCENE: LEARNING FROM THOTH

C: It's nighttime. We all go to our places and receive energy. It's my favorite time of the day. It is a time where I get to feel the oneness within and I am commencing with other philosophers, other astronomers, other beings that are coming to me to teach me in order for me to teach others. I like the quiet. This lifetime is very quiet. It is...there are energies of Tehuti, who is the Great Alchemist. He holds the Emerald Tablets. He holds so many soul embodiments, such as Melchizedek, Nostradamus...many, many incarnations of beings. He has many soul essences. On my end, we connect through, not words, but energy, philosophy. I feel Nostradamus. I feel the numbers. I feel the Mother Mary energy. I am more of the transmuter of the energy. Tehuti is the astronomer download. It is a very great kinship healer. Healer, friendship, as he and I have created magic, and that is what the time was about...it's about magic. Creating what is unseen from knowing...from a "knowing"...you must believe it to see it, and that was such a great and useful tool and is now a tool that is being reintroduced. The tool of manifestation.

NEXT SCENE: HOLDING THE LIGHT

C: In the temple. Sitting next to my partner in front of people. He has something in his hands. A gold staff. It looks like a snake. Actually, it's not a snake. It's a lion on the top of it — a lion's head. It keeps the energy away. It's a protector. He keeps it facing the people.

M: So, what are you guys doing there in the temple?

C: Guiding.

M: How do you guide?

C: Energy. The priestesses have their hands out to receive the energy. I am sitting next to my partner. My hands are facing the people. I'm not saying much.

M: How do the people look?

C: They're all in white. They're barefoot. It feels like worship, an initiation. It's before the underground.

M: What happens there?

C: The actual underground school where there isn't worship, but there is the inner knowing of finding God within. I keep getting the word Thoth.

M: What about him? Is he there?

C: Yes, he is the information. He's holding a tablet of information that I also received a lot of knowledge from, the Emerald Tablet. And Thoth is important. He's just showing the tablet. He says to bring in the bird knowledge. Use bird medicine. Very important — it's a way to open the heart chakra. Pretend the soul is in flight but hold steady to the Earth. He keeps pointing his hands at me, so it feels like we don't speak a whole lot; we just exchange energies and downloads.

NEXT SCENE: SITTING UNDER THE STARS

C: It's beautiful. Up high. It's got a white bed, and I have many women there working, and they keep it beautiful. They keep it together for me (gentle laugh). I like it at night. Most of the time I channel the stars for healing properties and study astrology. Tonight, I am connecting with a wizard.

M: What does the wizard teach you?

C: Alchemy.

M: Does he have a name?

C: Melchizedek — sacred geometry.

M: What kind of things do you learn from him about sacred geometry?

C: Everything's interconnected. It's the magic of manifestation. The light frequencies pull energy. So starlight is a very good time to manifest. I sit at night by the pyramid and hold my hands up. I sit in a receptive position with legs crossed. My palms are facing upward, resting on my lap. That's how I get my downloads.

M: So, you just open yourself to the stars?

C: Yes.

NEXT SCENE: SITTING WITH THE COUNCIL OF RA

M: I want to learn about the people that you live with. Let's go to a time where you're all sitting together for a meal. Be there now. Tell me what's going on.

C: It is joyful. There are eight chairs. Everything is stone. And we're all wearing white, and there's a lot of gold.

M: What do you look like?

C: I have very green eyes, dark hair. I have a headdress on and lots of paint on my face.

M: Tell me if there's anyone sitting there at the table with you?

C: It's a tribe of people. The women are on the left, and the men are on the right, and my partner is across from me, so I'm at one head of the table, and he's at the other. There are three on one side and three at the other. I'm at the front, and my partner's at the front.

M: What's your connection to these people?

C: Council.

M: What kinds of things do you see over?

C: The Egyptian people.

M: What do they call you in that council?

C: Council of Light, but I also hear the name Ra.

M: What do they call your body and your person in that lifetime? Can you hear that?

C: Isis (she pronounced as ee-sis).

M: Is there anything else you would like to share?

C: Animals. There is knowledge in the animal. There was a lot of esoteric wisdom drawn from animals. They played a very important role in guarding the temples, so I am very close to my animals.

M: How would you gain esoteric information from the animals?

C: They are a part of our totem. They are a part of us. They are our soul family as well. They are the guardians. They have the power of presence. They have the wisdom of the unseen. As for Tehuti, the Bird Tribe carry within their totem a bird essence. He, as well as I, knew that whether you had the totem of a swan or a heron or an eagle or any sort of bird, it was a true honor to have that in your totem. Others had felines; others had cows; and others had dogs. These beings we do not consider less than us. They weren't even animals. They were teachers. We did not own them. The priesthood is getting together. The high priestesses are coming in. It is a beautiful gathering. Some queens do not enjoy these gatherings. I enjoy them. There are souls from different star systems coming to this planet to learn. There are people coming from different areas from Earth to learn from this temple.

M: What kind of things will they learn?

C: Manifestation, instant healing, vibrational frequencies, healings, downloads. They are learning the esoteric art of alchemy, the meaning of existence. They are learning philosophy. They are learning many things.

NEXT SCENE: DEATH OF OSIRIS

C: There's chaos. People are running. Not sure what they're running from. I'm standing at the front looking out.

M: You're in front of what?

C: The temple. Yes, there's...(breathing) I'm just getting the word disbelief. Hathor and I are turning to each other and are holding each other, holding energy to send out to other people. The council is sending energy out.

M: Why are they sending energy out? What's going on there?

C: Unrest. Something is missing.

M: What's missing?

C: A leader.

M: What happened to the Pharaoh?

C: Killed.

M: Who would have done such a thing?

C: His brother. Set.

M: So, what are you doing now?

C: Praying. Holding the energy among sisters and brothers, but the people don't understand.

M: So, you hold this energy, and what happens next?

C: Get guided to go.

M: Where will you go next?

C: Find the Pharaoh.

M: Ok, so tell me what happens next?

C: Go to the Nile. See he's dead. Thoth is there, and we guide in the manifestation of magic, of burying the energies of the Pharaoh.

M: Tell me how you do this?

C: Intention and the Emerald Tablet.

M: The Emerald Tablet is part of it?

C: Yes, it's a big part of it.

M: And so, you connect with the Emerald Tablet?

C: And magic and manifestation happens. It's the unseen, the unknown — letting the manifestation happen — magic happens. His Earth body is done, but he's resurrected, and all of the work that we've just done worked out for the Pharaoh. He's living but in an ethereal body.

M: How are things with the people?

C: They want revenge.

M: Revenge against whom?

C: Set. I don't agree. It's not worth the energy.

M: What do you think would be the right choice — the highest choice?

C: Having an heir.

M: Like a child? So, what happens?

C: Yes. Thoth says it could be done through the ethereal body, that I could have a baby, and the people will calm.

NEXT SCENE: CELEBRATING WITH THE COUNCIL

C: There is a council meeting. There is a council. It is almost a celebration happening.

M: What is the celebration about?

C: My son. He is becoming the king. Everybody is dressed up in a very proud... There are many people who will be influenced by him. We keep walking through the tunnels, and everybody's hands are up. We are speaking without words. At the end of the tunnel, we go into a beautiful, beautiful room where there is a table...a long table where all of the brothers and sisters sit, and a celebration happens. Many, many, many nonphysical entities, as well as my sister. There is my husband, who is there. There are three chairs on the left, three chairs on the right. The front end has beings across the table.

M: What do you call your husband? What is his name?

C: *Osiris. It's interesting. We are each wearing different headpieces that represent our specialties. Yes, there is one with a snake on the top of the head. The snake is the conqueror. It is the infinity sign, but the conqueror of ego and emotion. It is a sign of royalty. A lot of us are wearing some sort of snake jewelry, but I see that headpiece very clearly.*

M: So, a snake, and what else? What else is on that headpiece?

C: *It is gold and black. It looks like the sphinx...what the sphinx looks like. Only certain people can go near the knowledge that is in the sphinx, and the Gnostic knowledge is there as well. It is very much tied into Jerusalem and the Essenes. It is a sign of knowledge —The Keeper of Knowledge. There is a lot of laughter and joy, and the energies are so comfortable that there is no trying. My son is to the right of me, and he is now able to wear the wonderful eye makeup that is announcing him as a part of the spiritual council. It's very bright and light and joyous and fun.*

Hathor is also somebody that I go to often to laugh and enjoy. She is the bringer of laughter and dance. Dancing is very, very huge in raising the vibration of energy. In Egypt, there was a lot of dancing and celebration. Movement. There was knowledge of movement. There were schools but knowing that we were all there as Christed beings, as Source consciousness, as Bird Tribe, Star Tribe members, it was a very fun time to experiment with vibrational frequencies and being in human form.

My child is being crowned. I see his crown — I see the back of his head. He's eight or nine. Horus. He's taking over. People are rejoicing. It's a sacred time. He has his father's staff. He's wearing a white robe to his knees, and he's barefoot. He is being adorned with things, and the people are sending beautiful energy to him. The sky and the Earth have finally come together.

M: What do you mean by that, "the sky and the Earth have finally come together?"

C: *Merging the Sun energy and the Earth energy in my son. He's just walking forward. We're sitting again in the same temple and its [an] initiation.*

M: How do they initiate young Horus?

C: *Adorning him with things. Also, he's given the visions and that is how the sky and the Earth are merged. He is opening up to the visions that he's ready to see.*

NEXT SCENE: TRANSITION OUT OF LIFE

C: I see the sky, and I'm on my bed. It's Sekhmet to the left, Hathor to the right, and my son is there. I feel very, very honored. I feel very empowered and rested and I can see that I am older, and the sisters would also help keep my room, keep my temple, my room upstairs. They were my best friends; they were my maids, and it is time to transition. It is very, very peaceful. No one is crying. It is not the mourning that we do here on this Earth plane. It's just as natural as birth, going into a new realm, ascending. It is something that can be done while living as well.

Many people in modern times have a draw towards Ancient Egypt because they lived lives there in preparation for this modern life. Let us reawaken the temple magic of Egypt and celebrate our eternal spirit. Let us each become a pyramid of Light upon this planet and beam the frequencies of Remembrance out across our beloved Gaia. It is time to remember our ancient codes of Ascension!

NINE

Holographic Earth & Planetary Grid

S acred Geometry is the foundational template of Creation formed by harmonic structures of Light and Vibration. Everything within Creation is formed using this divine coding and language.

Earth exists as a holographic field of overlapping connective pathways of light and sound formed in sacred geometric design. Flowing telluric currents of electromagnetic life force pulse information and evolutionary coding across the vibratory field that we call Earth. These pathways have been called different names by the ancient Indigenous and wisdom-keeping cultures of the world, such as ley lines, dragon lines, songlines, and dream tracks. Along these subtle energy lines, we find rivers, lava flows, mountain ranges, currents of weather patterns, and pathways of migratory animals. All of life is connected in symbiotic relationships through these etheric, vibratory highways of subtle energy.

Pyramids

One of the biggest mysteries is the pyramids that are being found all over the world in areas like Giza, Bosnia, Mexico, Guatemala, Australia, Indonesia, St. Louis, the Grand Canyon, and off the coast of Japan under the ocean.

In the ancient days, the Builder Races from the stars and higher realms built pyramids and star technology structures upon the Earth to support healthy, progressive evolution across the biomes of Earth. Thirteen major pyramids around the world create a system that receives, converts, and transmits evolutionary coding across the ley lines connecting with pyramids, temples, stone circles, and other sacred sites across the planet built by several generations of humans and nonhuman beings.

These pyramids line up with other pyramids and energy pathways in distant star systems as part of a fractalized information superhighway interconnecting all of Creation back to Source. Three main star points that our planetary grid system connects with are in the constellation of the Pleiades, Orion, and the star system of Sirius A and Sirius B. The global pyramid system acts as a bridge for the higher light dimensions to infuse Earth with higher evolutionary coding to evolve the entire matrix of Earth.

The building of these structures was systematically coordinated and developed in particular timelines and areas of the Earth in preparation for these times we are living now. They had to be created in a way that humanity would believe that they could build them on their own using manual labor. I have pyramid building stories from the Inca, the Olmecs, and a few from Ancient Egypt that all describe the stones of each of those pyramid systems being moved into place using forms of telekinesis, materialization, alchemy, and divinely inspired harmonic geometric design. I do believe that humans tried to build them on their own at later times, but the architecture is noticeably less precise and stable.

I am told that the capstone will be replaced fully when we are in the New Earth frequency and that the energetic structure of it is being put in place now as we prepare for the next stages of Ascension. This will put what was described as a "gel" over the grid of the Earth to assist our ascension. This will help with telethought communication and regulate the electric influxes that are occurring from space weather, the Schumann Resonance, CERN, and other causes. This will help with cardiac health and the psycho-emotional purges from the influxes.

More and more pyramids and star technologies will be found in the oceans, frozen within the ice, underground, and in other hidden places in the coming years. I am sure this will accelerate as public disclosure of the truth of extraterrestrials increases. Each of these "discoveries" is timed for when humanity is ready to receive such revelations at each stage of the ascension process.

Sacred Sites

At certain points within Earth cycles, higher levels of energy pulse from the planetary grid. Full moons, new moons, solstices, equinoxes, and other celestial alignments mark shifts in the global vibrational signature. New energies come into the planetary system and pulse through the planetary grid and vortex points to support harmonic evolution across the biomes of Earth. These time markers are potent opportunities to implant intention into the planetary grid to affect collective consciousness and planetary evolution.

The ancient Indigenous and wisdom cultures had various methods of connecting with and manipulating these pathways in practices that some call geomancy. Sacred sites like temples, stone circles, sundials, and megalithic structures were built by ancient people along these pathways or at intersection points where subtle energy pathways converge and pool, creating swirling vortexes of Light information. Ancient priests, priestesses, shamans, and initiates would gather at the sacred sites and power points to communicate with and travel to other realms, anchor prayers and blessings for their communities, share gratitude for the Earth, and manipulate weather patterns, among many other uses.

In ancient times, temple priests, priestesses, and medicine keepers would clean and clear the sacred sites. These ancient initiates knew the power of the sites and regularly held ceremonies and sacred rituals to amplify divine energies and intentions. These sites serve as multidimensional portals, where you can access information from other realms. Large communities held ceremonies and celebrations at the turning of the seasons and during astrological events to anchor their prayers of love and awakening and transmit their intentions to the higher realms and ancestral lineages.

During the Dark Ages, much of this was forbidden, and many died because of their sacred work. There are groups of people in every period — some sisterhoods, some brotherhoods, some a mixture including nonhuman higher intelligence species — which met at these sacred sites to initiate, activate, and clear energies. Many of us have been called to do this work on the Earth now. During my travels to sacred sites worldwide, I have had incredibly powerful experiences where higher dimensional energy poured through my crown and radiated out into my energy field. During these powerful transmissions, I have received insight and wisdom for the next stages of my life and self-healing in parts of my being that I could not access before visiting the site.

The Druids and pagan traditions of the UK, Ireland, and Europe have extensive systems of ley lines and sacred sites. I have had some of my most powerful experiences along the Apollo/Athena ley line, which is sometimes called the Archangel Michael ley line. This line of energy runs from Skellig Michael in Ireland through the tip of the UK, France, Italy, and Greece and passes through Mt. Carmel in Israel, where one of the Essene mystery communities was located.

The ancient wisdom traditions and Indigenous cultures are stewards of the planetary grid and have been in service to maintaining harmonic exchange across the system for thousands of years. The history of colonization can be seen at these ancient sites as dominating forces have condemned native spiritual traditions and built over their sacred sites with their structures and enforced new dogma on the people.

The esoteric knowledge around the amplified ability to manifest during certain gateways is known by both positive and negatively polarized groups. As we approach major holy days and astrological alignments, fear and chaos-generating events are coordinated by negatively polarized groups who wish to hijack the opportunity for expansion to keep humanity in the lower consciousness states.

The awakened people of the world are invited to anchor in heart-centered intentions and visions during these times to amplify unconditional love and unity with the Divine and this blessed Earth. As carriers of Light, we are invited to anchor divine presence upon the Earth and to project visions of peace and wholeness during these gateways while those who are not awakened are likely to be swept into the entropic mind control trap set up by service-to-self groups.

The war on consciousness is real, and it has been happening for quite some time. Wars over land and resources include the fight for power over the grid of consciousness. There is a major stargate in Iraq that souls exit the Earth plane from on their way back to Source. Another major vortex is in Jerusalem at the Temple Mount, the land of Megiddo, and around St. Catherine's Monastery in Sinai where Moses is said to have received the Ten Commandments. One session showed the connection of the black cube in Mecca which is said to transfer siphoned energy from Earth to Saturn to be used by nefarious star beings. Many vortex sites are owned by institutional Christianity that broadcast distorted teachings of Jesus, Mary, and the Disciples from these powerful sites, programming fear, shame, and condemnation into people's hearts and minds, thus suppressing consciousness and making humanity slaves through their perverted teachings. Clock towers were used to keep us programmed into linear time versus eternal creative experience. Military complexes have been built on the sites, pulsing fear and war mentality into the field. One of the grossest energy vortex sites I have been to is the Pentagon. Cell phone towers built along these lines pulse harmful electromagnetic frequencies across the planet, creating a cage-like environment for our hearts and minds.

For example, I have visited many sacred sites along a ley line that travels from the UK to Denmark that many call the Mary Magdalene line or the Michael-Mary line. At one site close to Copenhagen, I stood looking west down the ley line pathway, looking at the miles and miles of church steeples that were built on the line. The ground that I stood upon contained two ancient ceremonial burial grounds desecrated by decades of public executions. Next to me, on the same piece of land, stood a military tower with various broadcasting devices attached to it and a cellphone tower broadcasting cellular signals. This is just one example of how convoluted the grid has become.

When Jesus and Mary walked the Earth, they traveled to many grid points to anchor in new codes and dismantle the "dark matrix" established by service-to-self beings. These beings overlaid the "fallen consciousness grid" over the Earth grid which used the inherent dual nature of third-dimensional consciousness to their advantage. This saturation of "fallen thoughtforms" was used to hijack human consciousness by overpowering the mind and subtle vibrations to keep people in endless cycles of reincarnations. Many starseeds have been completing the work on the grid since the first wave arrived starting in 1945. As the starseeds move about the planet, they create a new grid for Gaia's energy to be cleared and act as lightning rods for new energy to come in. Much of this work is done unconsciously as starseeds are called to travel to different locations around the globe to shine their love! Thank you starseeds for taking on this grand mission!

One of the most recent technological attempts to suppress consciousness is the global installation of 5G satellites, Wi-Fi routers, and smart meters. It has been said over and over again in sessions that these frequency devices are not good for humanity. It is advised to detox the body of heavy metals, get into nature more frequently, move away from 5G towers, turn off Wi-Fi broadcasting systems, and turn off the smartphones as much as possible. These attempts to control human consciousness are futile as we are now ascending to a consciousness that cannot be affected by these measures. Over the coming years, all of these harmful systems will collapse as the new harmonic structures are put into place. We will take them down!

Interacting with the Planetary Grid

At this time, many are being called to different sites and ley lines worldwide to either receive codes or play some part in the restoration and reactivation of these sites. As the planet's energy ascends in frequency, these sites are emitting beautiful energy that can be interacted with. Many beings want to be on or near Earth just to feel these new energies! It is like an orchestra of musical spheres toning the songs of New Earth! I highly recommend traveling to the places you feel called to travel to. You never know what magic that land has for you.

We interact with the planetary grid primarily through the Earth Star chakra and our heart center. In this way, we are connected to the life force of Gaia and all information from her past, present, and future. Each moment, we act as a bridge between the higher realms with the planetary grid. Starseeds and lightworkers are moving across the globe, cleaning and clearing the grid consciously and unconsciously as part of their divine service in this life. This is why many of us prefer not having a solid home base and choose to travel the Earth and visit sacred and beautiful places.

When traveling to a sacred site, I feel that the site begins to work with your consciousness before you arrive. Often, Ron and I would have some type of argument as we drove to the site. Unknowingly, subconscious lower energies were being cleared to prepare us for the sacred grounds. As we traveled to the sites, often repeating number sequences (e.g., 11:11, 1:44, 2:22) and other synchronicities would happen en route to the site.

Before entering a sacred site, it is important to ground, center, and tune into your energy field. Some of these sites are quite powerful. Sometimes I would get dizzy or disoriented, or manically joyful. Each site is unique in its energetic offering. These ancient sites have often become popular tourist sites with a cacophony of etheric, emotional, and mental, energies congesting the site's vibratory field.

When at the site, I recommend starting with a meditation to connect more intimately with the energies. We are often barefoot at the sites so that our nervous systems and energetic pathways interact with the site's matrix without being hindered by shoes. Simply ground, center, and drop into a place of absolute stillness.

I have experienced a full spectrum of events when it comes to these sites.

Some are so congested and dense from tourists that I did not want to stay long. Other sites were like stepping into another world while high-frequency energy pulses through my body and floods my energy field. Each experience is unique and beautiful in its own way.

Many sacred sites of major historical importance are treasured and adored by the people who protect them. Many sites belong to Indigenous people. These sites should be treated with the highest respect. While traveling to Australia, an Aboriginal man explained his hostility towards people visiting his tribe's region because of uranium mining and the defacing of important ancestral sites. In many places, it is suggested to get permission from the lands' custodians before entering a sacred site. Whatever you are guided to do, do it with love in your heart and respect.

Leaving an Offering

While many people leave items at sacred sites as an offering, I find this eventually becomes a mess of wet and weathered items polluting the site. Plus, depending on the stewards of the land, offerings could be seen as disrespectful, vandalism, or littering. I once met an Aboriginal man who said he would try to get my visa revoked if I even chanted on the land!

I suggest leaving something energetic. Sing a song, dance a dance, shine your love, or some other activity that brings the energy of joy and gratitude into the vortex of the space. Simply coming with heart-centered intention and an open heart is more than enough to show your gratitude for the site and Spirit. I honestly feel the best offering to give is your silence, your listening, and your loving presence. Just BE there!

Transcript: Andromedan Builders of Incan Pyramids

Here is another session transcript from a somnambulistic client named Krissa. It took me some time to comprehend the massive story that was unrolling because there were so many plot twists! I did this session back in the beginning days when I practiced QHHT. There are several topics in this one session that were shocking and new for me. Looking back years later, I am seeing several opportunities to get more data. I am always hungry to learn more about all of these lost and hidden stories.

C: *Beautiful valley, but I'm in pain in my neck because someone's tied a rope around my neck. I hate them.*

M: **Tell me what else you're seeing there. It won't be uncomfortable. You can just allow that to be more comfortable now as you tell me what's happening there.**

C: *It's getting more comfortable. These men are there. They're not like us. They have these animals and spears, and they see that I have magic or power. I'm a woman, but I'm really, really tall. Taller than them. They're scared of me. They have a rope around my neck, and they're pulling me going somewhere, and I don't know where.*

M: **What's it look like around you? What kind of place are you in?**

C: *There's a jungle; there's a river. There are our buildings of stone. Oh... I see I'm here, but I'm not from here. This is...we call it South America now.*

M: **Why don't you look down at your body and tell us what you notice about your body. You said you're a woman.**

C: *Yes, pretty much. The people I'm with are small and brown, and I'm tall with red hair, and I'm very white, and they know that I came from a ship. They're not afraid. They put me as a sage, or a wise woman, a wise medicine person. I'm not a regular human. I'm having a hard time remembering where I came from exactly, but I know that when I think about it, I'm sad. I want to go back (begins crying). I want to go back (continues to cry). I don't like these humans that much. Why did I have to do this?*

The Spanish and Portuguese came, and they want gold. They're killing people, and they want to keep me. They tied a rope around my neck, and they're putting me on a boat. I can't help the people who are getting hurt. I'm planning to kill myself.

M: **Before you do that, you said you have powers. What kind of magic do you have?**

C: *I can put my hands on people and pull their sickness out of their body. Transform it and heal them. I can wave a...oh, I'm seeing it now...(laughs). I can wave a geometric light grid around their body.*

M: **What does this light grid do?**

C: *It can be for healing and protection. It can be around a place. Oh, I can see something interesting. There's a lot of places those Spanish people didn't find. One kind of this grid thing can make a place cloaked into invisibility, not totally, but less likely to be noticed. That's nice. Wow. Oh, I can see what's happening...*

People who are getting killed let fear overcome them. They're not staying in these temples that I made. I told them if you stay in there...I went out there and let myself be captured as a distraction. I'm taking the heat on purpose. I'm trying to tell the people to go back into those stone temples that are protected, but they run out in fear, and that's why they're getting killed; it's the fear. I'm trying to tell them, "No. Stay in the frequency of love, and you'll be protected. Go into those refuges that we made." But they're doing the best... They don't know. They're just really scared. It's terrible what's happening. These people are Spanish, and they don't even think they're human. They're treating them like nothing, like animals, and even animals shouldn't be treated this way. It's disgusting. And they're just looking for gold and resources and slaves. And I don't know what they're trying to do with me, but they are scared of me. They have a metal ring around my neck.

M: When you say you built these temples, how did you build them?

C: It's the sound. Oh, there are others like me...I can see them now. I'm not the ultimate master of building in sound, but some of them can do it with sound and harnessing those powerful tools that use crystals and sound. And the builders in my race set these, but I set the grid protection around them. They can move stone with sound and crystals. They can really do it. I think they can lift and levitate these... Oh, I see, I just showed somebody to put a capstone on using only the power of your mind.

M: Do you all call yourself anything?

C: Oh...Andromedans.

M: Andromedans. And what about the people you're with? These shorter people. What do you call them? What do they call their tribe?

C: I'm being shown that today we call it "Inca." There's another group I encountered, the Toltecs. Very wise, very beautiful and wise. But I was mostly with the Inca.

M: Ok. Tell me what's happening now.

C: I'm on the ship, and we're going...and they think that they're really going to get a lot of money from me because I'm different and have these powers. But they're keeping me below, out of the sun. All I eat is fruit. I live on (fruit) and sun. They're giving me this weird paste. It's disgusting. But I could go for a very long time without eating food. I'm not very worried. It's uncomfortable. I realize I could take my own life, and I was almost planning it, but I saw another way.

M: What's the other way?

C: *I saw that I could create a storm and shipwreck, but I found compassion for them, and I decided not to do it. I decided not to create a shipwreck and a storm. I decided to trust. Not the humans...and that's okay. But I decided to trust myself and my people that whatever happens, that nothing will happen that is beyond my capacity. So, I'm on the voyage, and I'm kind of smiling now. I have dropped deep into a meditative state. Almost like stasis. I'm glowing.*

M: What are you doing when you're in this state? What is the purpose of it?

C: *Energy conservation and union with love and Source. Something like the connection to receive downloads from the mothership. It's not just a ship, it's a center of love and community. That ship feels more like home than anywhere on Earth. I can see the whole ship. It's like I can directly connect in that state. My brainwaves are so slow. I'm a pure channel.*

M: What was the purpose of you coming to the planet? The Earth?

C: *I did volunteer for it. Elevation. Illumination. Laying groundwork. Setting some foundations of a conduit for more light, higher consciousness to come in. This particular group was one of many that were focused on from a number of groups. I'm seeing another ship with beings from many star systems that I've lived in. I just see my body morphing and changing like a big fast forward. It doesn't matter how I looked in these different places and different bodies. At the core, it's the same being, and it's a really loving, ancient being, and we were setting up elevated consciousness on the planet. There has been so much, what we would consider human, [that] had influence from other planetary systems, but the Andromedans were on a council and Galactic Federation, and some of us are real masters of healing, sound, energy, color, and light. We were setting up civilizations with the knowing. I didn't get to help them become adept before this interference with the conquerors, but wow, they had the potential to learn. These humans have the potential to learn...and it brings joy. They do have love. They can feel so much love.*

NEXT SCENE: DRUIDS

M: What's happening?

C: *I made a big escape. Someone was trying to hurt me to get information. They don't understand the information. They didn't believe me, and so I made myself nearly invisible, and I was able to sit in stasis to the point where the physicality of my body was not as solid anymore, and I slipped right now off the shackle on my neck. They were so shocked and confused. It was almost funny. They couldn't believe it. They couldn't believe it, and some of them really felt like idiots, and too bad! But I got away...I'm seeing a boat, but where is it going?*

M: You're on the boat now?

C: *This is a different boat though now. I got passage somewhere else. Okay...it's colder and very green. The people there...*

M: What about the people there?

C: *Oh...there are some who are very wise and intelligent. I'm seeing the stones, plant medicine, and they know a lot about the celestial bodies. There's a group.*

M: What do these people call themselves? You can hear this now.

C: *They said a word in old Gaelic and said the modern word is Druid. I'm doing something with a crystal where I look through it with my eye, and I can look at a woman and tell her who she should mate with, have children with, to fortify her bloodline. I'm stewarding the development of these people. Wow, I really have this open connection with the ship now, and these people know that I came from the stars, and they also are fine with it. Some people were very open back then...my mind is moving so fast; I need to slow it down a little.*

M: Tell me what's happening as you experience it.

C: *I'm teaching these people and learning from them. And there were beings over there before. I know them, Pleiadian beings...Lyran ancestor. I've had lifetimes there too. So much more emotional than the Andromedans. We can be passionate but years of refinement.*

M: So, the Lyran beings are more emotional?

C: *Yes, but very, very wise. The ones who are emotional...there are these younger strain of Pleiadians who once Lyrans were. I'm seeing the Pleiadians...I don't want to say factions, but some are more evolved than others. I don't want to be rude, but some are more evolved than others. Some of them have a more feline look, but they aren't a feline being, per se. They're just a little intense, a different frequency. But the Druids have a deeper understanding, and I can see that some of these people...*

I can see this is now called Wales, and some of these Welsh people ended up in Australia, and this bloodline really took root down there. When I sit in stasis and connect to the ship, I'm reminded that most of my mission on the planet is just being exactly who I am. Not trying too hard to do any one thing because I would get sad sometimes. What happened in South America made me very sad. But that I was doing my purpose just by being and carrying a frequency not native to the planet but really loving, beneficent, elevating. Not so much about doing but being.

M: What makes Wales such a location for everyone to gather?

C: It seems like the veil is thinner there for some reason, and there is a powerful crystal aspect in the land.

M: Tell me more about this.

C: Jesus. There are two things. The bloodline of Jesus ended up in Wales at some point. I can see that glowing, like a thread through the land, yellow-gold, white-gold...beautiful...Christ bloodline. But then, some crystals from Atlantis ended up there. The word Avalon keeps coming up... What is that? I can't see what it is...(exclaimed). I saw something funny! Merlin is real. He's a real person!

M: What else are you seeing there?

C: Tower on a hill. No...that's somewhere else. Gosh, I'm seeing grid lines lighting up, connecting to powerful spots.

NEXT SCENE: CHRIST BLOODLINE

C: I'm holding a little baby. The baby was having trouble feeding, and they brought the baby to me. I'm a healer. This is in a similar place. The baby's skull bones and spine... I can place my hand on them and make subtle adjustments. The flow of the fluid, the baby is healed; I hand him back.

M: How do you work with this energy? How do you bring it in?

C: I open a portal at the top of my head. I quiet the mind and the senses, and it flows out through my hands. Oh, my gosh... this is a child very close in the lineage of Christ. I'm supposed to support this lineage. It's showing me something. Jesus Christ was from a ship. Oh my...

M: Tell me what you're seeing as you see it.

C: I almost want to cry...how wonderful. The star of Bethlehem was really a ship!

M: Tell me about it. What do you see there?

C: Beautiful, advanced Pleiadian ship of Light. And it wasn't that the baby...that's how Mary got pregnant. It was time. Everything we did before...it's showing me multiple lifetimes of setting the stage so that such a baby could be born right at that time. The divine...everything is so misunderstood.

M: Set the record straight. Tell us what we need to understand.

C: All of our enlightened masters and deities are examples of beneficent, loving extraterrestrials who have come to elevate us. To elevate us! That's the salvation! And Christ was a living embodiment and example, but when he said, "We will do all of this and more," he meant it. He meant that humans will reach the point of being able to do things like he did, like I did when I was living on the earth closer to my Lightbody form. We don't need to feel so limited by the heaviness and density now. This planet has so many seeds of Light from different extraterrestrial races that are here to benefit us. Yes, there have been negative influences, but what I'm seeing now is...it's not even worth talking about. It's so inferior now that it's not even worth talking about — the negative races and negative influence — because there's so much light that's about to reach a critical tipping point. And the fact that I held in my hands a baby of the lineage of Christ and he just needed a little adjustment in his spine...sometimes our spine things are just not flowing quite right through that channel, through that energy channel. I'm moving my spine now. There! Sometimes all it takes is a little adjustment to keep flowing properly.

M: So, what are you seeing now?

C: I'm seeing myself growing old in that lifetime. I had to look human enough in that body, but I was quite old.

M: How old did you live to be in Earth years?

C: A little bit over 200 Earth years in that lifetime. I'm going off into the woods, and there is not a death experience that happens. What I'm seeing is that...it's so crazy. I'm sitting at the base of a big tree. I'm cozy and warm, and I'm going into a deep, deep meditation. The energy of the tree, I can see it now, is wrapping around me and through me, and I'm becoming lighter and lighter. I've been still for weeks and months. The body, the vessel, shrinks down, and there is an explosion of Light upward. And my consciousness is gone, back to the Source, just in this glowing, peaceful light. The tree helped carry me home. It's so beautiful.

Closing Statement

This session has many keys to unlock lost knowledge and trigger cellular memory for awakening. Hopefully, I will get to work with this client again in the future to research more of this storyline. Many components of this story are revisited through other clients in later transcriptions that are in this manuscript.

TEN

Avalon & Jaguar Shaman

A few clients have gone back to the lost matriarchal civilization of Avalon. They describe a highly psychic community that honored the Divine Feminine principle of the Godhead. The Avalonians worked with the fairy and elemental realms and were very connected to the Earth's living waters. As the shadow consciousness of the world descended on the region of Avalon, the Druids helped to fight against the intruding forces. The Avalonians decided it would be best to ascend to a higher dimension and assist from the higher planes.

Transcript: Journey into the Mists of Avalon

As Gaby came into the scene, she describes herself as a female wearing a blue, hooded dress with a golden cord around the waist. She is standing in the forest, holding a round magical object in her hand that resembles an eye that illuminates her inner vision. She has a strong connection to the trees that surround her and feels that they are "holding space." She lives in a temple space illuminated by crystals in a community in nature. Joyful children are running about having fun. The community eats lightly, mostly fruit. She spends most of her time swimming, meditating, and connecting with a tree. She also spends a lot of time sitting in deep meditation and quiet presence with other community members in a sacred circle.

C: *I am human. A woman. I am sitting with children, teaching. I feel that I am teaching everybody, and I am channeling and connecting to the Source. All these kinds of tools. Two kids, I feel that they are girls.*

M: **What kind of place are you at? Look around at your environment and describe it to me.**

C: *It's a temple surrounded by water. It's beautiful, kind of like an antique Roman temple with white stone and with lots of light. And I see water all around. It's very peaceful. Light.*

M: **So, you're teaching the children in this temple?**

C: *Yeah, and I see the women walking around. We are all in blue. It's a blue skirt and a blue dress with large sleeves around the arms. It's very soft and beautiful.*

We are all barefoot.

M: Do you have a name for this temple?

C: The only thing coming is "Avalon." I feel that I am hosting a circle of women.

M: Describe to me what is happening there in the circle of women.

C: It's how we communicate and how we discuss and see how we can serve best. It's very flowing telepathically. Everyone is sharing what is important that needs to be said and being heard in return. I feel there is something with the outside world.

M: What's happening in the outside world?

C: I think we feel what is coming. There are men outside, Druids, that we can communicate with, and they are the ones who are witnessing and are immersed in it.

M: What are the Druids communicating to you?

C: That our past is ending. Our time is ending. They do their best, but they're saying there is a disconnection now and they can't hold it anymore. They are asking for our help.

M: And what will you do?

C: That's why we are in a circle. We are putting our energies together to send light and love.

M: Tell me about that process. How do you do that?

C: By intention. We have our third eye open; that's why we have the symbol on our forehead.

M: Describe the symbol to me.

C: It's a moon, the crescent moon, holding the third eye. So, it helps focus and direct...

M: So, you sit together and focus your third eye somehow? How do you do that?

C: Yeah...from the divine. We are all connected to the Divine. And then, through the third eye, we hold the Light in the middle. This Light ball which works with Earth. And the Druids are able to receive, to channel, but not the human.

M: Why not humans?

C: They're closed, and it's okay. It has to be.

NEXT SCENE: HEALING WATER

C: I can't feel my legs. I see water. I feel like I am paralyzed until my knees. Maybe I'm in the water. Yes, I am in the water.

M: You're in the water, wonderful. Describe it to me. What's around you?

C: I don't remember the word in English. It's not cloud, mist. Fog and mist.

M: So, you're in the mist. Why are you in the water?

C: (Sighs) We need to. We have to leave. It feels this way to live is not safe anymore. The energy isn't safe anymore. We can't hold the Light anymore. There is much darkness. I see fire. I feel like it's destroyed what we've built. Our safe temple has been destroyed. Humans. They don't understand. They don't understand what they are doing. It's sad. We are grieving. We can't do anything anymore. It's another time. We were all connected to Mother Earth, to the trees, to the water, we were one. It's nothing now.

M: Times are changing?

C: Yes, and it needs to happen. It's okay. We have done everything we could. We have learned what we needed to learn. Our time has passed. Now, I feel it's in a body now. We need to learn through the body. It's hard. It has to be to come back. I think we have become too light, not enough in our body. We need to go back to the beginning to learn to be in the body. We are leaving peacefully now. To the Light.

M: So, you're going into the Light now?

C: Yes, but it's not death. We keep doing what we're doing, but from another place.

M: Take me with you and tell me what's happening as it happens. Describe it all to me.

C: I dance with the water. I am going through the water.

M: You are going through the water? How does that process work? Tell me how it happens.

C: I feel like the body had to emerge slowly. That's why I couldn't feel my legs. But now (pauses)...it's hard to describe. We're all going in at the same time. Kind of going through a wave.

M: And everyone is doing this together? How does it feel to do this?

C: Light.

Transcript: Life of Goddess Rhiannon of Avalon

The client named Norah describes herself barefoot with a long, white dress and cape on and she called herself Rhiannon. She lived in a forest cottage with her horse and had a healing bed with crystals that she used for her healing work with the community which she called Avalon. She described the birth of her child who was born with a crescent moon on her forehead just like her mother. This marked them as Priestesses of the Goddess who carried the Light teachings upon the Earth.

In this next scene, she is with a group of women in a secret, invite-only meeting at Stonehenge, working with the magical energies of the Moon. The women are setting up for a sacred ritual honoring the Goddess.

C: *There are only thirteen of us. The older women are setting up. Some of us are going to receive. Mmm. We're receiving something tonight on this full moon. I'm not sure of what yet. Someone is placing a wreath, or a headpiece, on me. It's made of flowers. And she just handed me a crystal — an amethyst crystal. She's asking me to hold it during the ceremony against my heart. She kissed both of my cheeks. There are thirteen roses.*

M: **What does the number thirteen symbolize for you?**

C: *It's a sacred number of the Goddess. We celebrate thirteen moons, thirteen cycles of the Divine Feminine, to honor our bodies. We honor our cycle [menstrual]. We honor emotion. We understand that with the moon we can release the emotions and honor them at the same time. It's healing.*

M: **Do you often meet in this way?**

C: *We meet on the full moon and new moon. We're all healers. We all have healing abilities. Many of us bring something different, and we honor each other. We teach each other so that we all can learn from one another.*

M: **What healing abilities do you work with?**

C: *There's a white light coming out of my hands. And my heart — the energy is gold. It is to heal. It enters through my crown and goes through my body. Others use herbs and can create potions, elixirs...elixirs they're saying...elixirs. Some balance energy. There are those that "see." So, they bring what they see for whomever, and in their knowing they know what needs to be done, and then they send them off to those who can do the appropriate healing. So, we all work as one.*

M: **So, everyone gets to use their unique gifts to work together.**

C: *We are one. We don't separate ourselves. We are the energy of the Divine Feminine in individual form on Earth. We come together, and we share all that we have been given and all that we know. And we pass this on, if we have daughters, we pass on this knowledge. We are not the only group of thirteen.*

M: **What other groups are there?**

C: There are other sisters that do this as well. I'm seeing three groups. They come from far. They use the same grounds. They don't have it there — the ground is very sacred. It's a connection point. There is, below, what looks like a crystal cavern or maybe a mine. It's very high energy and high frequency. We know it's there — others don't. The sun and the moon energize the area. It almost looks like the crystals are a battery, and when the energy of the moon comes in, the full moon, the energy shifts. And you use that energy for...I'm seeing twenty-four hours; you have twenty-four hours to use this energy of the full moon. It cleanses those of us that do this work (sigh of recognition). This is a cleansing ritual. It's because we work with others and we remove their illness or injuries or density, we have to remove it from our own selves. The full moon does that in this particular space. Ah! It's amethyst below us. It's very healing. That's why it's sacred. The Sun is out. It charges through the Earth, and it reaches the crystals. There is a way to get to the crystals, but only a few know how.

M: How do you access the crystals?

C: There is an opening...this is not the same place where the original stones were. It's been moved. To access from where we were.

M: You said they moved the stones to access more of the energy?

C: No, this is the original place where we're at now. They were moved...they're not in their original place anymore in this time.

M: So how do you find the access pathway for the crystals?

C: There is a drop-down cliff that is all stone. We know where it is. You have to be small to get in. It's on the side, what they're showing me, it's on the side of this stone ledge or mountain. And there is a path at the edge, it's very narrow, and we walk it. And there's an entrance, but only...you would have to be a woman. It's too small for men; they can't get in. They've tried. So, a child can get in, or a small woman. We go in sideways. You don't even know it's an entrance to anything; it's very well hidden. We turn ourselves sideways and we push against it, and we slide in (sigh). There is an energy there as well, where when you get to a certain point if you are not pure of heart you will not be allowed to enter. It's beautiful in there. We perform rituals there.

LAST SCENE OF HER LIFE

C: They're telling me I don't leave in illness. I leave in the Light. I chose to pass on the knowledge to her today. After I pass the knowledge on, I'll step into the

Light. So, I won't be there.

M: Will your physical body experience death?

C: No.

M: How does this process work?

C: It is our choice to leave. As eternal beings, we can step into this Light. It's an activated Light that comes from above when we are ready. It's done when we step into it.

M: Well, when you're ready, you can step into this Light.

C: I told my daughter I will see her in the Light one day. It's purple, just like the amethyst.

M: Purple Light?

C: Yes. I am being lifted. The Light is taking me straight up. It is gold. My body is just traveling...it is stopped.

M: Where did you stop?

C: Home.

M: Home, mmm. What does home look like?

C: It looks like the sky.

M: Are there others there?

C: I'm stepping out of the Light. Yes, there are many here. It is a celebration when you go home. You may choose to leave the body and allow the soul to leave, but some of us just step entirely into the Light when we know our work is done. Mmm. There are many.

M: Very good. I want you to now be with your counsel of guides and other high beings. Be with them now and tell me what's happening.

C: Mmm, they are greeting. Saying "very well done." There are many.

M: What kind of space are you in?

C: I'm a room, and the table is round. There are twelve here. They are all wearing (chuckles)...they're wearing the same stuff that I see in meditations. It is like a white linen with gold at the collars. And a gold sash. It is very comfortable. Some of them have a long tunic with pants, but some of them just have a long robe. Some of them choose to wear an open collar and some of them choose closed. It is all white. The gold is around the collar, and the sash is gold.

M: What are the names of the beings that are there? In your counsel?

C: Many of them are masters. They are guides. Jesus is there. Mother Mary, Master Kuthumi (laughs), Melchizedek, Athena, Rowena. There's the mother, Isis.

They are saying, "Council of Light." They are the Council of Light.

M: **They have important information to share with you. Connect with them and tell me what they share.**

C: *What you set out to do has been accomplished. The process continues.*

M: **What was it that you set out to do?**

C: *To heal. Each dynasty is a culmination, an ascension process for humanity. It's gone both ways. They're showing a blueprint of Gaia. That's why the table is round, it covers the entire table. It's the blueprint of Her. It shows culmination points they are saying. It shows us dense points and points of light. It shows what needs to be focused on. Where the Light needs to reach. Where the healing needs to go. And why there are those of us that have to go. We take our beacon of Light there; we bring the codes in, and we anchor them. We anchor them under Earth, into the crystals. We spread this energy of Light until it reaches another that is doing the same thing. Until it covers the entire Earth. It's bringing back the Light of life force energy. It had been blocked. It was shut down because it was not of the Light. It hurts my heart (almost starts crying), what they did...*

M: **What did they do? And who are they?**

C: *The negative energy. The dark forces. They took our light for their own. They feed off of it. They feed their...(sighs)...it energizes a structure of theirs. I do not understand what they're showing me. They use the crystals. They use the crystals the wrong way. I am hearing nuclear fusion. Atlantis. They used the crystals the wrong way.*

M: **Was the dark structure there in Atlantis?**

C: *We had structures there we placed in the beginning. We used them in temples. The temples were mounted over highly energetic areas. We infused those crystals with the energy, the same way I did in that lifetime. We infused them in love and healing. There were other ones that were used as energy centers. They were batteries. There were certain ones that were batteries to power ships and to bring power to what we needed. But the others came and manipulated the power. They changed it.*

M: **What did they do to change it?**

C: *Dark magic. There became more of them than there were of us. They wanted the power for greed.*

M: **What did they do?**

C: *They took over the centers. They were able to manipulate the energy. Some...these beings are different; they're not like us.*

M: How are they different?

C: You can feel their energy. You can feel their negativity. I don't like it. It's making me sick. Ugh.

M: What happened there in Atlantis to cause the cataclysm? You can see it now.

C: It looks more like a nuclear war. It's...I see what looks like beings from ships, but not beings of light...beings of conductive energy, beings of negativity, beings that blow things up. They're blowing things up. Fighting on the ships. This isn't how it's supposed to be. It's not what we originally created in the beginning. It's not the same. It hurts my heart.

Conscious Death

The mysteries of ascension and conscious dying are sacred arts taught only to the highest initiates in different orders on and beyond the Earth. I have had other clients describe spinning their cells faster and faster until they became Light, ascending through pillars of Light, or consciously laying down to leave the body. This potential lives in ALL OF US. As we grow in our attention and tend to our Divine Light, the Mystery is revealed by the Master who lives within, and we awaken to our immortality.

Transcript: The Jaguar Prophecy

Another lost civilization that was brought through in an IQH session was a jungle culture that had medicine people who were able to shift into animal forms. The high priest of the culture could take the form of a powerful jaguar. This position was passed down to the fastest young boy in the tribe. The high priest carried a staff that could be cracked against the Earth to make the ground shake and the jungle animals ROAR!

C: There's a woman crying. She is in pain. She's about to give birth.

M: Why are you here?

C: I am singing. I have a rattle.

M: What are you singing?

C: I am calling in the jaguar. I am getting old, and there has not yet appeared a young man in our tribe who is capable of receiving the power of the jaguar.

M: What happens if there is no young boy?

C: *That is why I am calling the spirit into this child. The mother is in great pain. When she gives birth, it is not a human child. It is a baby jaguar.*

M: **What does this mean to you?**

C: *This was foretold by our people. For thousands of years, there has been a prophecy. When a jaguar child is born into the people, a new threat is coming.*

M: **What is the new threat?**

C: *When we hear of the men coming across the water, we must leave our cities because these men come to destroy us. We will go back to the jungle. Those who have not forgotten will survive. Those who can shift shall remain in their animal forms.*

M: **What else does the prophecy say? How long must you hide?**

C: *Thirteen. My people will not know the cities again.*

M: **What does the number thirteen have to do with this?**

C: *Thirteen cycles before our lands are free.*

M: **How do you measure one cycle?**

C: *It is where the sun rises on a certain day of the year. This moves over the years, but when it returns to the point where it shines its light on the pyramid, it is the beginning of a new cycle.*

M: **So, it will be thirteen of those before the freedom of your people again?**

C: *There will be freedom, or there will be the annihilation of all.*

M: **Tell me more about this prophecy. Is there more information, more to the story? You can even share the full thing if you'd like.**

C: *At the time the jaguar child is born, there will begin the great scattering of our people. The stories will arrive of strange men from the far waters. Men with hair on their faces. These men come to destroy our people and to take our land, and this cannot be prevented. At this sign, our wisdom carriers must train as many as possible. Transmit the wisdom and the powers and strengthen our connection with the jungle. The cities must be abandoned, and we must roam with the jaguars in the jungle. Many of our people have forgotten, and they will not survive. We shall remain in the consciousnesses of the jungle. These strange men will change many things. As we watch, we shall not recognize our land. And for thirteen cycles, we must wait. At these thirteen cycles, these men with hair on their faces will destroy themselves. If the land shall remain, we may emerge from the jungle and build our cities anew.*

<u>Generation of Prophecy Being Fulfilled</u>

While many may doubt these stories, I have come to believe that anything is possible and that I just need to open my mind to understand the bigger picture. In all these scenarios of collapsing society, the cause for these civilizations to fade into history was the rise of service-to-self consciousness where people abused power for their own personal gain. We are the generation that puts this struggle to rest! We are the ones who get to see the end of domination, overlord power structures, and heartless destruction born of ignorance of our True Nature. We are the generation that learns to walk and live in honor of all levels of Life. Let us claim our bodies, our communities, and this planet for the Light, and welcome in this new Era of Peace and Harmony!

Now, let us journey into the Cosmic Christ Transmissions!

ASCENSION LEXICON

I have put together a list of words commonly used in this book and for the topics of awakening, spirituality, and ascension. These are not necessarily defined this way by others but are an excellent way to understand my writings in this book in a more clear and multidimensional way.

-A-

Adamic Form: Original perfected divine human form created for highly developed Light Beings to experience physical creation from within the physical dimension. Fourth Density (4D) body of the New Earth human connecting with oversoul consciousness, higher dimensional beings, and telepathic species.

Agartha: Ancient Inner Earth multi-species civilization with its own sun and ecosystem within the Earth. See *Inner Earth*.

Ain Soph: Kabbalistic term for Source before manifestation into form and translates to "Without Limit" as it is the unlimited creative potential behind all of Creation. Same as "Ineffable" in the Gnostic texts. Can also be written as "Ensof."

Akashic records: Higher-dimensional spiritual records of all experience past, present, and future. Each soul has one. So does each planet and so on.

alchemy: The application of spiritual knowledge to matter to create transformation. This is more commonly known with the Middle Ages' pursuits of turning simple metals into gold. High alchemy being the alchemy of soul/lightbody.

Ancient Egypt: Last golden age of Gaia when many beings held 4th, 5th, and 6th-dimensional consciousness before the descent into lower consciousness (forgetting).

Andromedans: Highly advanced star beings from the Andromeda galaxy assisting humanity's ascension.

Anunnaki: Star beings from the Nibiru system. Sumerian space "gods" who manipulated humanity for personal gain. Now most are in support of humanity's ascension.

apocalypse: 1. Greek word for "unveiling." 2. The dismantling of the mind control matrix and false projections from the controlling forces to reveal to humanity the ugly underbelly and karma of the collective consciousness upon the Earth from this creation cycle which is to be fully reconciled before the planet changes in dimension to Fourth Density New Earth. Not the "end" but a transitionary phase into the next creation cycle.

Archons/Controllers: Term used to describe negatively polarized service-to-self, nonphysical, intelligent beings who siphon negative energy from humanity for their own gain using mind control tactics to keep humanity enslaved through fear and distorted consciousness. The controlling forces behind global institutions. Will be fully dismantled before the shift to New Earth.

Arcturians: Star beings from the constellation of Arcturus assisting Earth with Ascension.

Ascension/ascension: 1. The spiritual maturity process of a soul, moving from an unawakened state of mundane consciousness to multidimensional Source/God-realization described as the movement of the kundalini up the central channel, samadhi, moksha, nirvana, salvation... 2. The movement of Creation into greater states of Glory. 3. The current collective planetary transformation from 3D to 5D consciousness and the New Earth reality.

ascension symptoms: Physical, etheric, mental, and spiritual changes during ascension cycles. Includes headaches, emotional purging, detoxifications symptoms, multidimensional DNA reprogramming, body aches, vivid dreams, and beyond.

Ascended Master: Level of spiritual hierarchy of beings who have ascended in their consciousness enough to no longer need to incarnate in form for spiritual growth but may choose to incarnate to assist the ascension process of a species.

Atman: Divine origin identity, True Self, True Nature, the Witness Consciousness of a lifestream. Same as Brahman. Source Self. Eternally free.

aura: Electromagnetic field of subtle energy that surrounds and pervades the physical body. Contains ever-shifting patterns and geometries of light and vibration that create the template for the physical form.

-B-

biotransducer: organic instrument for transforming energy information for the purpose of manifestation and communication with the universal hologram and divine frequencies. Able to utilize advanced intelligence and spiritual information for the transformation of reality in the human environment.

bodhisattva: Sanskrit term for someone on the path of Buddhahood (ascension) who dedicates their path to the liberation of all beings from cycles of suffering. Able to achieve liberation but delays to assist others in consciousness expansion.

Brahman: The Absolute Reality. Source in impersonal, nonmanifest state. Pure Infinity Existence Consciousness Bliss, *Satchitananda*.

buddhi: the Intellect, reflected consciousness, enlightened consciousness in each person.

buddhic consciousness: enlightened consciousness expressed by *buddhi*, the vehicle for the soul, experienced as profound intuitive insight, unity, and bliss.

-C-

Cabal: Global elite network of negatively polarized service-to-self operatives and organizations working towards complete domination of humanity and planet Earth. See *Archons*.

causal consciousness: the higher mind capacity which utilizes soul memory and intuition to observe and understand manifestation multidimensionally.

centering: Alignment with one's divine nature and inner truth, activating a bridge between Gaia and the Divine through the heart center.

centropy: Regenerative electrification of matter-energy.

chakras: Spiraling transformers of subtle energy with seven primary vortices emanating from the central channel (*sushumna*) which govern our perception of the projected holographic reality and energize our mental and physical processes.

channeling: Opening one's consciousness and vessel as a conduit for subtle energy or other consciousnesses.

Christ: 1. Yeshua ben Joseph (Jesus) in his ascended Lightbody. Forerunner of christ consciousness as part of a divine plan for redemption and restoration of humanity and Earth back to a 4th Density collective. 3. A collective consciousness field that has many emanations and incarnated forms throughout the history of Creation. 4. Title given to one who has achieved consciousness mastery and is "anointed" by Light.

christ consciousness: Also called cosmic consciousness or 5D consciousness. Demonstrated by Jesus of Nazareth in his resurrected 4th Density body.

Christ/Magdalene Lineage: Genetic implantation of higher DNA coding through the offspring of Jesus and Mary. Descendants are worldwide and able to carry a higher light quotient and awaken more easily.

clairaudience: Clear hearing is the ability to hear messages from your Higher Self or spirit beings. This includes hearing the thoughts of other people.

clairgustance: Clear tasting is the ability to receive intuitive information through the sense of taste.

clairesalience: Clear smelling is the ability to intuit information through the sense of smell.

clairvoyance: Clear sight is the ability to perceive information through internal imagery.

clear channeling: Mediumship, or spirit channeling, is the ability to communicate with nonphysical beings and consciousness structures. This can include souls who have passed beyond the veil of physical life or beings that exist in other dimensions.

collective: Representing an entire group, i.e., human collective.

Collective Messiahship: The unification of ascending humanity with the intention of global restoration and ascendency.

cords: Subtle energy attachments that connect us to other beings. Can be negative if developed through limiting beliefs and distorted conditioning.

council: Group of beings joined together with a common focus (i.e., your spiritual council of guides who support your spiritual maturation across lifetimes).

Councils of Light: Groups of advanced spiritual beings that govern the evolution of consciousness and the biological forms of a certain experimental zone to encourage higher states of glory and harmony with the highest being the Universal Council of Light.

-D-

density: 1. Mass per volume. 2. Bandwidth of consciousness reality.

Descension/descension: To go down. The forgetting or falling asleep phases of consciousness. The stepping down of light frequency.

dharma: The noble path of awakening guided through alignment with the Divine through one's True Nature. Exemplified by the life path of beings like Jesus and the Buddha.

The Divine: The frequency emanation that governs and sustains all of Creation across many universes within universes. God Source and the Hosts of Heaven. See *Godhead.*

Divine Androgyny: Harmonic synergy between the divine masculine and divine feminine energetic expressions that results in perfect balance and cohesion.

Divine Creatorship: The birthright of a human to create their life with free-will choice in alignment with their Inner Source.

Divine Feminine: 1. Nurturing creative quality of the Divine 2. Archetypal, spiritual, and psychological ideal of the feminine energetic expression.

Divine Masculine: 1. Administrative quality of the Divine 2. Archetypal, spiritual, and psychological ideal of the masculine energetic expression.

DNA: Genetic blueprint for the development of an organism with both physical and subtle components. Ascended humanity will have 12 fully restored strands.

-E-

Earth Changes: Physical and subtle energetic changes that occur on the planet as it prepares to shift into the next creation cycle. Includes pole shifts, weather changes, seismic and volcanic activity, electromagnetic shifts, and more.

Elohim: First Creation. Creator beings with individual consciousness that work in groups to form Creation. Some created as service-to-all working in unity with Source. Some were created as service-to-self permitted to create in the illusion that they were separate from Source.

empath: Individual who is sensitive to the subtle energy such as thought, and emotional projections of others as they intuitively feel the mental/emotional body of others within their own mental/emotional realm. See *clairsentience*.

End Times: The closing of this current creation cycle where all karma must be balanced, and all shadow revealed so that Earth and spiritually activated humanity can begin the next creation cycle in 4th Density New Earth. See *apocalypse*.

energy: Subtle energy beyond the visible light spectrum ranging from pervasive to neutral to regenerative and life-enhancing. Everything is energy.

energy awareness: Perception of subtle energy in and around one's body.

energy matrix: Geometric organization of subtle frequencies that creates the base structure for the development of form.

entity attachment: Astral debris that has attached itself to a weakened energy system of a host as a source of sustenance and a way to live out "unfinished business." Quite common and easily resolved most of the time by a trained spirit releasement practitioner or energy medicine practitioner.

entropy: Decay and degeneration of matter-energy.

extraterrestrial: From outside of the Earth's biosphere including other planets and universes. There are countless species in our solar system, galaxy, super galaxy, and beyond. Infinite species in infinite realms of creation with many advanced civilizations with histories tracing back trillions of years.

evolution: See *Higher Evolution.*

-F-

false prophets: Teachers and prophets who use spiritual information for service-to-self agendas. Many religious leaders, spiritual teachers, and even those in the ascension community will have their true intentions revealed in the final phases of Ascension.

Family of Light: Physical and nonphysical beings who live their lives in alignment with the Oneness of Creation and the Divine Source. Includes the races of the Star Nations who hold 5D consciousness and higher and the Hierarchy of Light who tend to the many levels of Light Creation.

5D: Consciousness of humans living on the New Earth, can be referred to as christ consciousness or oversoul consciousness.

4D: Awakening stage of ascension bridging mundane consciousness with the New Earth consciousness.

frequency: 1. Rate of vibration measured in hertz (Hz). 2. Higher vibrational rate is likened to positivity and centropy and lower rate towards negativity and entropy.

-G-

Gaia: 1. Sentient Earth 2. Common name for the soul of Earth. Also called Terra.

Galactic Federation of Light: Intergalactic and ultraterrestrial collective of advanced beings who tend to the evolution of consciousness and biological forms throughout the Milky Way. Comprised of advanced scientists, engineers, medical personnel, and other areas of expertise needed to maintain order and balance in the galaxy.

genetic implantation: Seeding of new DNA into the gene pool to evolve a species into higher states of harmony or functionality. Used by the Star Nations and Hierarchy of Light to craft zones of biological experimentation.

gnosis: Direct experience of divine nature through one's own inner being and inner knowing that leads to higher understanding of the nature of the divine reality. See *Knowledge.*

Great Central Sun: Source of all levels of creation in this universe. Brings higher evolutionary coding from Divine Source into other central suns in the universal grid which flow to each solar system evolving each region in accordance with a Divine Plan for Higher Evolution. See *Ishawara.*

Great Divide: The bifurcation of consciousness amongst humanity during the end phases of the planetary ascension process. Includes physical movement across the Earth as humanity moves to be with others of shared consciousness and similar vibration and soul path. Two-world-spit of those who hold negatively polarized, service-to-self consciousness and those of positively polarized, service-to-all consciousness.

Great White Brotherhood: More accurately **Great White Siblinghood**. Ascended Masters, human and non-human, of all gender expressions organized into different orders or councils who tend to the evolution of consciousness and sometimes incarnate to bring new teachings and new energy. Many of these Ascended Masters have aspects of themselves on the planet now to assist the Ascension.

Greys: Extraterrestrial beings from Zeta Reticuli.

God: 1. Supreme Source of Creation 2. Divine Masculine, administrative quality of Godhead, Eternal Mind. See *Ishwara.*

Goddess: 1. Divine Feminine, nurturing, regenerative, creative aspect of the Godhead. 3. Mother God.

Godhead: The Divine Consciousness Source and its various emanations and functions.

Golden Ages: Times of high consciousness and harmony upon the Earth during the Precession of the Equinoxes. (e.g., Avalon, Lemuria)

grounding: The anchoring of one's physical and subtle bodies into the Earth's core through intention, diaphragmatic breathing, and visualization through the Root and Earth Star chakras.

guides: Spiritual beings who assist an incarnated being on their dharmic path towards liberation.

-H-

hara line: Central pillar of light connecting an individual with Gaia and Source.

heart-centered: Action born from inner truth and spiritual ethics through alignment with one's divine nature.

Hierarchy of Light: Various levels of divine consciousness forms, aspects of Source that serve different functions in the evolution of Creation. Ain Soph/Source, Elohim, Archangels, Angelic Realm, Ascended Masters, Ascended Goddesses, Interdimensional Beings, and Restored Humanity in Adamic Form. The Hosts of Heaven.

Higher Evolution: Beyond biological evolution and natural selection, the recoding of experimental zones of the hologram of Creation using divinely encoded frequencies projected through the stellar network which are coordinated by benevolent beings, physical and nonphysical, who serve the evolution of the Divine Plan throughout the Multiverse. Also includes introduction of new genetic expressions into the gene pool, new technologies, and new ideas to be used to evolve the creation into higher order.

Higher Self: 1. The mature part of our consciousness which operates in positively polarized, service-to-all consciousness and is connected to our divine nature. 2. Sovereign self. 3. Harmonic Divine/Human synthesis. 4. Oversoul. 5. Atman.

Holding space: A term used in spiritual growth and self-development circles that means "to hold suffering in an alchemical container of loving awareness so that it may heal."

Holy Spirit Shekinah: The feminine regenerative energy of the Divine. The "presence of God" in the physical dimension. Opening yourself to channel the divine presence begins an alchemical process of light activation that heals and restores all levels of one's being.

-I-

Inner Earth: Ancient and contemporary subterranean civilizations. Many beings went to Inner Earth before the destruction of Lemuria and

Atlantis. See *Agartha*.

intention: Inner resolve to direct one's focus and creative capacity towards a specific goal. *Sankalpa* in Sanskrit.

interdimensional: Existing between dimensions.

intuition: The ability to perceive energy information beyond the five senses before it has become physically manifested in reality. 2. Extrasensory perception.

involution: spiritual consciousness activation that begins as one moves through Ascension and sheds the mind's conditioning.

Ishwara: 1. personal expression of Source. 2. Source in purest manifested form. Commonly called "God" 3. Great Central Sun. 4. Universal Logos.

-J-

Jesus/Yeshua ben Joseph: Master of Light for Earth. Twin flame of Mary Magdalene. Supreme teacher of Divine Love and Ascension. Brought restored DNA and pure Christ Light to the Earth to activate the 4th Density Redemption Plan. Yeshua's cosmic oversoul legacy includes many star systems including the high spiritual schools of Light in the Pleiades and Sirius A and B. His arrival into this dimension of space was the Star of Bethlehem Lightship. His life path was supported by many galactic beings incarnated upon the Earth as well as many extraterrestrials and ultraterrestrial beings. 2. Incarnation of Ascended Master Lord Sananda.

-K-

karma: 1. The sum of a being's actions in this life and in previous existences, both positive and negative actions which influences the soul's path through incarnations.

Knowledge: "Gnosis," divine insight that activates higher consciousness and God-realization. Sanskrit *aparoksha*

kundalini: Serpentine energy originating at the base of the spine that ascends through the sushumna during the awakening process creating ecstatic spiritual expression.

-L-

Lemuria: First advanced human civilization. Often associated with the Pacific Ocean. Destroyed by major flooding and earth changes.

ley lines: Subtle energy pathways that carry evolutionary information across the planetary grid. Also called dragon lines, songlines, telluric lines.

Light: Regenerative divine energy emanations that exist beyond the typical visible light spectrum (Holy Spirit). Different than conventional light from lightbulbs.

Light beings: 1. General term for nonphysical beings of divine origin. See *Family of Light.*

lightbody: 1. subtle body 2. Vital, lower, and higher mind sheaths. 3. Transmigrating soul

Light Conception: The act of conceiving a child directly from the spiritual realms without the need of sperm from a physical being.

Light language: 1. Language spoken through connection to the Divine Presence. Activates multidimensional healing and powerful internal experiences with healing frequencies. Gift of the Holy Spirit, the regenerative creative frequency that quickens and restores all levels of Life. Can be self-initiated or pushed through from the Higher Self and the Divine.

Light Seed: Higher-dimensional, light-encoded genetic material used for Light Conception and altering the genetic composition of a species. Aka *Immaculate Conception.*

Lightship/lightship: Divine craft made by one individual's lightbody/merkaba or a merged merkaba from more than one being for the purpose of interdimensional travel through space-time, stargates, and higher light realms.

Love: Beyond egoic love, unconditional love that is naturally expressed when one develops love for the divine and a service-to-all intention. *Agape* love.

lokas: Sanskrit word for the planes of existence.

loosh: energy of suffering and death harvested by negative human, extraterrestrial, and interdimensional beings which is used to fuel nefarious agendas.

Lyrans: Star beings from the constellation of Lyra. Most commonly known race is the feline beings. First humanoid race in the Milky Way. Original 144,000 oversoul starseeds to bring the human species to Earth.

-M-

magic(k): Use of universal, natural law, and intention to manifest. Can be either service-to-self (dark) or service-to-all (light).

manifestation: The materialization of intention into form.

mantra: Holy names and phrases repeatedly spoken or thought which generate divine thoughtforms to reprogram the physical, etheric, and mental bodies opening one's consciousness to higher perception, divine insight, and union with the Divine. Use of mantra repatterns the DNA, clearing distortion and debris and reprogramming it into higher order and functionality for the projection of divine consciousness light.

Mary Magdalene: Twin Flame and Divine Partner of Jesus. Ancient Egyptian Priestess. High initiate from the Pleiades, Venus, and other high consciousness realms. Arrived at Earth with Yeshua in the Star of Bethlehem Lightship. Gave birth to the offspring of Jesus. This lineage is spread throughout the world.

maya: Illusion. Projecting and veiling power of Source. All that has form and name which tests our ability to see the all-pervasive divine consciousness that supports all manifestations.

meditation: Conscious focusing of the mind on a single object.

merkaba: Divine light vehicle in the auric field that gives one the ability to travel to the higher light realms. Introduced back to humanity through Elijah.

Michael: Archangel who protects and defends all levels of Creation and biological life.

mindfulness: The practice of bringing our life's gross and subtle manifestations into the light of our awareness to observe life in nonduality. Nondual awareness is the ability to see beyond the illusion of duality and see with the eyes of loving awareness.

Mother Mary: Cosmic divine being, a Master soul, who incarnated to give birth to Jesus. High priestess of Ancient Egypt and master teacher of the cosmic priestess arts.

multidimensional: Existing in multiple planes of consciousness, i.e., physical, etheric, mental, and various spiritual dimensions.

Multiverse/multiverse: Universes within universes creating the totality of Creation. What Jesus spoke of when he referred to his "Father's house with many mansions."

-N-

nadis: Pathways of subtle energy in the body. There are said to be 72,0000 that weave in and around the physical body.

New Earth: 1. Higher density light spectrum reality of the ascended Earth. 2. Kingdom of Heaven on Earth.

nirvanic consciousness: liberated consciousness which has transcended suffering, limited egoic identity, and karmic cycles.

-O-

Orion: Constellation with ancient intelligent races with varying levels of consciousness and ranges of polarity. Factions of Reptilian and humanoid beings from Orion fought against Lyrans in the long galactic war.

oversoul: Higher consciousness identity of a soul. Where your individual soul comes from. Collective consciousness of myriad life streams and incarnations. 4th Density/5D Self.

-P-

past life regression: Form of hypnosis or shamanic journeying that evokes information from a client's subconscious mind from previous lifetimes.

Pleiadians: Star beings from the constellation of Pleiades, a highly advanced light consciousness school in our great universe. Cousins of humanity. They implanted upgraded DNA in humanity to open our spiritual connection.

prayer: Approach to the Divine through thought or word which opens the pathways for the living Light to infuse the one who is praying with love and divine insight.

priest: Male devotee of the Divine in service to the illumination of collective consciousness and the ascension of humanity. Administers the will and knowledge of the divine upon the Earth as well as the regenerative, healing presence of the divine feminine.

priestess: Female devotee of the Divine. Often connected to the Goddess. Embodies the wisdom of the divine feminine mothering principle of the Godhead. Matures consciousness in the community into higher states of creativity, sensuality, and grace.

psychic: One who has extrasensory perception. See *intuition*.

pyramids: Sacred architectural sites around the Earth built by various extraterrestrial and ultraterrestrial beings connecting the pathways of vital energy of the Earth with the universal energy grid for the reprogramming of life upon planet Earth. Act as broadcast and receiving systems for information used for planetary evolution.

Prakriti: Manifested reality, transactional reality as opposed to Absolute Reality, maya.

Purusha: Indwelling witness of Creation, Absolute Reality, Brahman, Pure Consciousness. Source Consciousness.

-Q-

quantum: Dealing with the holographic reality and fabric of Consciousness and creation.

quantum consciousness: Holographic consciousness connecting to the matrix of Creation with the ability to focus across time and space through nonlocality and consciousness projection.

quantum healing: Rapid, multidimensional healing that works at the cellular and subtle levels to bring the body's systems into homeostasis. Can be done through psychic processes, shamanic and energy medicine practices, hypnosis, quantum healing technology, star technology, and divine emanations. This is the medicine of New Earth.

quantum mysticism: Emerging evolutionary synthesis between science, metaphysics, and spirituality used to understand Consciousness and the laws that govern Creation.

Qumran: Ancient, multigenerational esoteric Essene community by the Dead Sea in present-day Israel that lived in complete recognition of the Divine through the study and embodiment of divine mystery teachings. Secretive community with advanced star knowledge and superhuman spiritual abilities. Traded knowledge with other global mystery schools and was home and school to Yeshua, Jesus of Nazareth. Yeshua's children studied here as well.

-R-

Reiki: 1. Japanese word meaning spiritual intelligence life force. 2. Intelligently-encoded, divine, redemptive, and regenerative energy from Source. 3. A gift of the Holy Spirit.

Redemption Plan: Cosmic and galactic initiative to restore humanity and Earth back to 4th Density as in the times of Lemuria. Includes genetic implantation, restoration of planetary grid, and operatives incarnating as human to bring new ideas and technologies, broadcasting intelligent and spiritual coding into the biofield of Earth and humanity, and more.

Reptilians: Reptilian humanoid star beings who have had a "negative" influence on Earth who have mostly evolved to positive polarity. Humans have reptilian DNA that gives us our ego mind to assist our perseverance in evolving.

reincarnation: The act of being born again into a new lifestream for the purpose of spiritual growth.

resonance: In spiritual terms, harmonic, synchronous vibrations between two or more objects.

Raphael: Archangel who administers to healing.

-S-

sacred sexuality: Alchemical sexual expression with the intention of uniting with the divine through one's own erotic spiritual nature. Can be practiced alone or with a partner(s).

sacred sites: Holy power spots spread across the planet that form a web of vortex points for subtle energy pathways of the Earth.

samsara: 1. Wheel of Karma 2. rounds and rounds of incarnations on the path of Ascension 3. Suffering mind. 4. Cycles of suffering.

samskaras: Grooves in the mind that create reactive emotions forming our biases, habits, and tendencies. Can be seen as negative or positive.

Self: Divine Self as opposed to the egoic self which is trapped in worldly conditioning.

sentience: The ability to feel, be conscious, or have one's own subjective experience.

service-to-all: Positively polarized, dedicated intention, thought, and action towards the Greater Good and Higher Love as an extension of one's True Self.

service-to-self: Negatively polarized, gives power to false self, ego. Can seem "positive" as intentions can be different than presentation.

sin: Intention, thought, and action that goes against one's inner light that causes an immediate depletion of life force and positive vibration. Serves the egoic self. There is no judgment for this from higher realms. All is for learning and growth. 2. Fear-based judgment system created by religion which connects to belief systems that limit the indwelling of spiritual light by creating perpetual states of fear, shame, and guilt. 3. The fundamental illusion of separation from Source.

Sirians: Star beings from the region of the Sirius A and Sirius B binary star system who have a long, positive history with humanity and are assisting Earth now.

Solaris: Central sun and stargate of our solar system which emanates supraliminal coding for the evolution of the myriad lifeforms in our solar system.

soul: 1. Subtle bodies which transmigrate from one life to the next. See *lightbody.*

spiritual partnership: A relationship that is supported by the desire to assist one another in awakening and healing.

soul contracts: Pre-designed plan and agreements before incarnating for the balancing of karma to propel the path of liberation and ascension. Includes soul agreements between individual souls to play out certain catalyst roles.

soul purpose: Divine intention for a soul for its incarnation encompassing the themes to be explored and lessons to be learned throughout a lifestream. Generally, a soul's purpose is to awaken to Higher Love and Divine Truth.

sovereign: natural consciousness state of the Atman/Self/Inner Source. Human beings embody and reclaim sovereignty through involution and higher consciousness evolution. Able to have agency in all areas of life. Self-regulated. Self-governed.

stargate: Portal used for transportation between long distances and different dimensions.

Star Nations: Space-traveling intelligent species, some positive, some negative, some neutral in relation to humanity and the Earth.

starseeds: Visitors from other schools in the multiverse who have volunteered to live a human life to assist the Ascension of Gaia and humanity. Many of which have experienced ascension mastery in other lifetimes. The best ascension masters from the universe are here on the planet or around the planet in crafts at this time.

substratum: 1. Foundational, base material 2. Source/Brahman/Atman/Pure Consciousness.

superluminal: 1. faster than light

synchronicity: The meeting of two or more seemingly unrelated events or objects that come together in a meaningful way that could even be perceived as divinely coordinated.

-T-

timelines: Pathways of probable events. Infinite potentials and realities fractal out and converge at particular junction points in "time" where choice points exist for the next fractal offshoots of timeline potentials. We are currently moving with multiple timeline potentials for Ascension events that lead to one inevitable event, 4th/5th Density New Earth. Timelines are constantly in flux depending on personal moment-to-moment choices from individuals or the collective meaning the future is never "fixed" but is always in flux. This is the reason why some psychics see different potential probabilities playing out in the future.

3D: Standard human consciousness in its unawakened state, fear/duality-based consciousness which is heavily programmed and hypnotized by the false matrix, the conditioning of the world, and the mind control techniques from the Archons.

Elders: Highest divine council. Progenitors of all cultures in the multiverse.

Twin Flames: Emanations of the same oversoul who assist one another in Ascension. Often uniting at the end of karmic cycles to serve Consciousness. Most commonly thought of as two people in Divine Partnership, but there can be more.

-U-V-W-Y-

Unified Field: The hologram of Creation, the Quantum Field, where all energies and manifestations arise from connecting all through Source Consciousness.

ultraterrestrial: Beings from beyond the physical plane, higher density beings in higher density forms.

vibration: The invisible, subtle layers of matter that form the basic templates for physical reality through repetitive oscillation.

Wisdom: Insight into the Divine Mysteries of Creation and the Godhead that connects us with higher states of divine love and divine grace. See *Knowledge, gnosis.*

walk-in: Exchange of souls during an incarnation. Typically occurs when the original soul consciousness assigned to the body can no longer continue an incarnation from trauma or some other way of vital depletion. A fresh soul consciousness is brought in to accomplish a certain task. Frequently used to bring highly developed galactic beings into the Earth for mission-oriented tasks.

Yeshua ben Joseph: See *Jesus* and *Christ*.

Recommended Reading

The Three Waves of Volunteers and The New Earth by Dolores Cannon

They Walked with Jesus by Dolores Cannon

Jesus and the Essenes by Dolores Cannon

Between Death and Life by Dolores Cannon

Keepers of The Garden by Dolores Cannon

Five Lives Remembered by Dolores Cannon

Return of the Bird Tribes by Ken Carey

Anna: Grandmother of Jesus by Claire Heartsong

Light on Life by B.K.S. Iyengar

The Yoga Sutras of Patanjali (many translations available)

Living Buddha, Living Christ by Thich Nhat Hahn

Reconciliation: Healing the Inner Child by Thich Nhat Hahn

Peace is Every Step by Thich Nhat Hahn

The Path of Energy by Dr. Synthia Andrews

The Seat of the Soul by Gary Zukav

The Book of Knowing and Worth by Paul Selig

The Diamond in Your Pocket by Gangaji

The Magdalen Manuscript: The Alchemies of Horus & the Sex Magic of Isis by Tom Kenyon and Judi Sion

The Kybalion by Three Initiates

Aparokshanubhuti by Adi Shankara

The Upanishads

The Bhagavad Gita

Drig Drishya Viveka

The Keys of Enoch by J.J. Hurtak

Pistis Sophia translated by J.J. Hurtak

The Secret Doctrine by H.P. Blavatsky

Etheric Double by A.E. Powell

The Causal Body and the Ego by A.E. Powell

Regression: Past-life Therapy for Here and Now by Samuel Sagan

Entity Possession: Freeing the Energy Body of Negative Influences by Samuel Sagan

The Illumination Codex

THE ILLUMINATION CODEX
GATEWAY ONE

Ascension Initiation

KEYS FOR HIGHER EVOLUTION

Michael Garber

THE ILLUMINATION CODEX
GATEWAY TWO PART ONE

Quantum Origins

KEYS FOR ANCIENT COSMOLOGY

Michael Garber

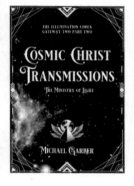

THE ILLUMINATION CODEX
GATEWAY TWO PART TWO

Cosmic Christ Transmissions

THE MINISTRY OF LIGHT

Michael Garber

THE ILLUMINATION CODEX
GATEWAY FOUR

Chakra Yoga Discourse

KEYS FOR HIGHER CONSCIOUSNESS

Michael Garber

THE ILLUMINATION CODEX
GATEWAY TWO PART THREE

New Earth Transmissions

FUTURE TIMELINES OF GAIA

Michael Garber

THE ILLUMINATION CODEX
GATEWAY THREE

Path of Awakening

KEYS FOR TRANSFIGURATION

Michael Garber

THE ILLUMINATION CODEX
GATEWAY FIVE

Laying of Hands
Reiki & Beyond

Michael Garber

WWW.NEWEARTHASCENDING.ORG

Support Our Initiatives

Ron and I have dedicated our lives to supporting this Grand Transition. We stand alongside all of you as humanity awakens to its True Nature and becomes a People of Light in the heavenly reality of New Earth.

New Earth Ascending is dedicated to assisting people to realize their divinity and manifest that truth in every aspect of their life. For more information about New Earth Ascending or to contact Michael, please scan the QR code below for a list of resources and links, or visit *www.newearthascending.org*. Be sure to check out our courses including the Illuminated Quantum Healing practitioner course.

New Earth Ascending is a registered 508 (c)(1)(a) Self-Supported Non-profit Church Ministry with a global outreach. We greatly appreciate your support as we create new systems, communities, and schools for the development of the New Earth civilization. If you would like to make a tax-deductible donation to support our mission, please go to:

https://donorbox.org/donationtonewearthascending

Scan with a smart device camera for more information including websites, social media, and more! Bless us all!

9 781959 561057